Sustainable Enterprise Strategies for Optimizing Digital Stewardship

LIBRARY INFORMATION TECHNOLOGY ASSOCIATION (LITA) GUIDES

The Library Information and Technology Association became part of Core: Leadership, Infrastructure, Futures, also a division of the American Library Association, in September 2020. Guides published in this series retain the series title LITA Guides.

Marta Mestrovic Deyrup, PhD
Acquisitions Editor, Core, a division of the American Library Association

The Library Information Technology Association (LITA) Guides provide information and guidance on topics related to cutting-edge technology for library and IT specialists.

Written by top professionals in the field of technology, the guides are sought after by librarians wishing to learn a new skill or to become current in today's best practices.

Each book in the series has been overseen editorially since conception by LITA and reviewed by LITA members with special expertise in the specialty area of the book.

Established in 1966 and integrated as part of Core in 2020, LITA provided its members and the library and information science community as a whole with a forum for discussion, an environment for learning, and a program for actions on the design, development, and implementation of automated and technological systems in the library and information science field.

Approximately twenty-five LITA Guides were published by Neal-Schuman and ALA between 2007 and 2015. Rowman & Littlefield and LITA published the series 2015–2021. Books in the series published by Rowman & Littlefield are:

- Digitizing Flat Media: Principles and Practices
- The Librarian's Introduction to Programming Languages
- Library Service Design: A LITA Guide to Holistic Assessment, Insight, and Improvement
- Data Visualization: A Guide to Visual Storytelling for Librarians
- Mobile Technologies in Libraries: A LITA Guide
- Innovative LibGuides Applications
- Integrating LibGuides into Library Websites
- Protecting Patron Privacy: A LITA Guide

The LITA Leadership Guide: The Librarian as Entrepreneur, Leader, and Technologist
Using Social Media to Build Library Communities: A LITA Guide
Managing Library Technology: A LITA Guide
The LITA Guide to No- or Low-Cost Technology Tools for Libraries
Big Data Shocks: An Introduction to Big Data for Librarians and Information Professionals
The Savvy Academic Librarian's Guide to Technological Innovation: Moving Beyond the Wow Factor
The LITA Guide to Augmented Reality in Libraries
Digital Curation Projects Made Easy: A Step-By-Step Guide for Libraries, Archives, and Museums
Library Technology Planning for Today and Tomorrow: A LITA Guide
Tech for All: Moving beyond the Digital Divide
Change Management for Library Technologists: A LITA Guide
Makerspace and Collaborative Technologies: A LITA Guide
Change the World Using Social Media
Information Technology for Librarians and Information Professionals
Creating Inclusive Libraries by Applying Universal Design: A Guide
Sustainable Enterprise Strategies for Optimizing Digital Stewardship: A Guide for Libraries, Archives, and Museums

Sustainable Enterprise Strategies for Optimizing Digital Stewardship

A Guide for Libraries, Archives, and Museums

Angela Fritz

ROWMAN & LITTLEFIELD
Lanham • Boulder • New York • London

Published by Rowman & Littlefield
A wholly owned subsidiary of The Rowman & Littlefield Publishing Group, Inc.
4501 Forbes Boulevard, Suite 200, Lanham, Maryland 20706
www.rowman.com

6 Tinworth Street, London SE11 5AL, United Kingdom

Copyright © 2021 by Angela Fritz

All rights reserved. No part of this book may be reproduced in any form or by any electronic or mechanical means, including information storage and retrieval systems, without written permission from the publisher, except by a reviewer who may quote passages in a review.

British Library Cataloguing in Publication Information Available

Library of Congress Cataloging-in-Publication Data

Names: Fritz, Angela, 1968- author.
Title: Sustainable enterprise strategies for optimizing digital stewardship
  : a guide for libraries, archives, and museums / Angela Fritz.
Description: Lanham : Rowman & Littlefield, [2021] | Series: LITA guides |
  Includes bibliographical references and index. | Summary: "As most
  institutions contemplate an enterprise digital content strategy for a
  growing number of digitized surrogates and born-digital assets,
  libraries, archives, and museums understand that these expanding needs
  can only be met by more flexible approaches offered by a multicomponent
  digital asset management ecosystem (DAME)"— Provided by publisher.
Identifiers: LCCN 2021006303 (print) | LCCN 2021006304 (ebook) | ISBN
  9781538142851 (cloth) | ISBN 9781538142868 (paperback) | ISBN
  9781538142875 (epub)
Subjects: LCSH: Digital libraries—Management. | Electronic information
  resources—Management. | Digital preservation.
Classification: LCC ZA4080 .F75 2021 (print) | LCC ZA4080 (ebook) | DDC
  025.17/4—dc23
LC record available at https://lccn.loc.gov/2021006303
LC ebook record available at https://lccn.loc.gov/2021006304

Contents

	List of Figures and Tables	ix
	Preface	xi
Chapter 1	Digital Stewardship and DAME Development: History, Definitions, and Concepts	1
Chapter 2	Assessing the Digital Asset Management Ecosystem: A Holistic Approach	19
Chapter 3	Digital Strategy: A Phased Approach to Building Capacity and Capabilities	35
Chapter 4	Integrative Collections Management: Streamlining Digital Stewardship	51
Chapter 5	Cloud-Based Digital-Preservation Storage: A Building Block for Sustainable Digital Stewardship	71
Index		89
About the Author		95

List of Figures and Tables

Figure 0.1	Components of a Sustainable Digital-Stewardship Framework	xiii
Figure 1.1	Understanding the Digital-Asset Ecosystem	7
Figure 1.2	Digital Stewardship Activities	9
Figure 2.1	Four Levels of Digital-Stewardship Assessment	22
Figure 3.1	Levels of Professional Development to Enhance Digital-Stewardship Capacity	46
Figure 4.1	Considerations for Designing Cross-functional Workflows	57
Table 4.1	Considerations for Digitization Paths	60
Figure 5.1	Example of a Tiered-Based Storage Strategy	79

Preface

For galleries, libraries, archives, and museums (GLAM), distinctive digital collections have the potential to transform research, learning, and public outreach and engagement in expansive ways. At the same time, the sheer size and fragile nature of these digital collections represent some of the greatest challenges for librarians, museum curators, and archivists who find themselves managing an increasingly complex ecosystem of digital assets. For the staff of most GLAM institutions, a digital ecosystem consists of a variety of assets, including digital surrogates of analog materials, research data, institutional records, open educational resources, digital exhibits, rich media, web-based and social media content, time-based art, licensed e-content, and born-digital manuscript collections. Due to the exponential growth of this digital content, most cultural institutions steward more digital objects than ever before.

Although the components of any digital asset ecosystem are familiar to most librarians, archivists, and museum curators, the scope and scale of this digital universe differs from institution to institution. The nature of any digital ecosystem is reliant on a number of factors, including the resource level and size of the institution, the scope and history of its distinctive collections, the robust nature of collection-development initiatives and electronic resource-management workflows, the research specializations of the institution, and the existence of an official mandate for a records management program and associated framework for information governance. Regardless of the organizational structure, which designates where digital-collection management, data curation, or digital preservation "lives" in an institution, all librarians, curators, and archivists are playing a greater role in the lifecycle management of enterprise content that encompasses stewarding digital assets from their inception to their discovery to their long-term digital preservation storage requirements.

Increasingly, GLAM institutions are managing digital-asset ecosystems by coordinating and consolidating a number of existing resources and personnel around evolving strategic digital-stewardship initiatives. These initiatives have emerged as GLAM institutions contemplate more unified information technology infrastructures to navigate enterprise challenges. With this as context, the goal of this book is to offer a basic framework to help librarians, archivists, and museum curators think *holistically* and *systematically* about digital-collections management. At its core, this guide underscores the importance of *purposeful uses of technology* in building services, strategies, and workflows around unified tenets of digital stewardship. This guide focuses on a digital-stewardship framework that supports digital-asset management at an enterprise level by aligning library acquisitions, museum registration, archival accessioning and processing, data curation, e-resource and metadata management, and analog and digital preservation through integrative collections management. This book presents a conceptual framework for building a sustainable digital-asset management ecosystem with discussions on digital-stewardship assessment, digital strategies and prioritization, and the critical role that foresight planning plays in balancing an evolving technological infrastructure with creative cost modeling and sustainability digital initiatives.

With the understanding that digital stewardship is a long-term investment that requires institutions to "build out" capacities and capabilities over time, the chapters build on one another and follow a logical sequence. Each chapter represents a distinct component of a digital-stewardship framework that can be scaled as necessary. The distilled components of a sustainable digital-stewardship framework include: holistic assessment, digital strategy and organizational realignment, integrated collections management, and tier-based cloud storage. As background information, chapter 1 establishes some key definitions of digital stewardship, outlines the history of the digital-asset management ecosystem (DAME), and explores the significance of an institutional mandate, the contours of information governance, and the importance of collaborations that reinforce an expansion of traditional boundaries for innovative partnerships and digital advocacy.

Borrowing from the principles of data curation, responsible digital stewardship begins with an understanding of an institution's digital ecosystem of licensed content, research data, digitized material, and unique born-digital content in order to ensure strategic growth of collections in the context of long-term holistic collection management plans. Chapter 2 offers a holistic, multilevel approach to digital stewardship assessment which encompasses an internal environmental scan of digital collections and infrastructure, collection and tool mapping, and, more granularly, digital asset inventories. This chapter also offers a multiple-method model for interpreting assessment data as well as a review of associated matrices for data analysis and prioritization, cost modeling, and assessment reporting. As a progression from stewardship assessment, chapter 3 focuses on digital strategy and organizational realignment as an essential component in expanding stewardship capacities and capabilities. Topics include reenvisioning GLAM organizational structures, implementing new leadership frameworks and approaches to digital project teambuilding, as well as conceptualizing professional development as an essential strategy for organizational realignment.

Building on previous sections, chapter 4 illustrates how digital stewardship assessment and digital strategy provide the roadmap for the implementation

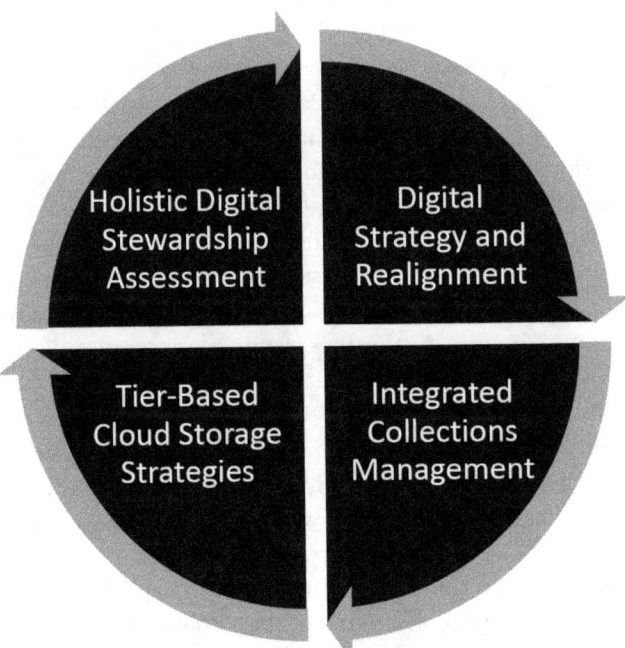

Figure 0.1. Components of a Sustainable Digital Stewardship Framework

of integrative collections management. At the heart of digital stewardship, this chapter discusses cross-functional and "curation-ready" workflows, the importance of a unified digital preservation strategy, and models for cost-effective approaches to "building-out" digital capacity and capabilities that are in line with an institution's digital strategy. The final chapter is dedicated to the foundation of sustainable digital stewardship with an overview of digital preservation storage requirements and cloud-based storage strategies. This chapter outlines the benefits and challenges of cloud-based storage including security concerns, pricing models, and hidden costs, as well as advocates for the adoption of tier-based storage strategies that are flexible, scalable, and sustainable.

This book has broad appeal across libraries, archives, and museums as many institutions contemplate digital preservation infrastructures, storage strategies, and organizational realignment to navigate enterprise digital-stewardship challenges. Not only does this book give readers a framework with a special focus on purposeful uses of technology, but it brings together a digital-stewardship service model that is designed to support the individual needs of the institution while highlighting the interrelatedness of digital sources and the importance of collaborative approaches to content creation, access, and preservation in the form of integrated digital collection-building across the GLAM sector.

More importantly, this book situates the framework for digital stewardship in the context of shifting landscapes, evolving skill sets, transformations in technology, and new organizational models with a greater focus on cross-functionality and collaboration. With a greater emphasis on data curation and digital-asset management, librarians, archivists, and curators are being asked to think holistically and engage in macro-decisions relating to infrastructure development to ensure interoperability, scalability, and sustainability of a universe of digital assets housed and maintained within their institutions. As most institutions devise an enterprise digital-content strategy for a growing number of digitized surrogates and born-digital assets, GLAM institutions understand that these expanding digital-stewardship needs can only be met by a flexible, modular infrastructure and associated collection management workflows that will allow them to "pivot" and "build out" with emerging technologies, as well as evolving digital content and fluctuating resources.

The primary goal of this book is to empower GLAM staff to become "good stewards" of these collections as they engage in multiple decision points, which include tool selection; the design, development, and creation of cross-functional workflows; policies and work plans; infrastructure development; evolving skill sets for managing descriptive, administrative, technical, rights, and preservation metadata; as well as understanding distributed digital-preservation models with a growing array of associated options for cloud storage. Due to the evolving GLAM landscape, the common theme of this book underscores the critical need for institutions to invest in digital-stewardship teams within and beyond their institution. These cross-institutional, interdepartmental partnerships are not only central in achieving innovative, technology-based approaches where digital-asset stewardship occurs alongside traditional analog materials but these partnerships are also the key to building the capacities and capabilities for an integrative collection management approach for digital-collection stewardship that is impactful and sustainable.

CHAPTER ONE

Digital Stewardship and DAME Development

History, Definitions, and Concepts

In order to plan for adaptable services around a digital-stewardship framework, libraries, archives, and museums have found themselves embracing more participatory, collaborative, and distributed networks, making greater use of digital technologies within, across, and among other GLAM institutions. At the center of these initiatives is a digital-asset management ecosystem (DAME), which is a concept that facilitates data management of the myriad digital assets created, maintained, and preserved by an institution. A DAME is based on a distributed service architecture that is designed around a collection of applications, tools, and hardware deployed through modular collection-management components that meet the complex needs of enterprise digital collections. This basic infrastructure facilitates the integration of preservation, accessibility, and discoverability of a range of digital assets by merging traditional collection-management actions and processes with principles and methodologies of data curation, digital preservation, and information management. With a DAME, digital assets can be shared at an enterprise scale in order to encourage the use, reuse, and remixing of assets for different stakeholders while safeguarding institutional memory, administrative continuity, and cultural heritage.[1]

Toward A Digital Asset Management Ecosystem: An Evolving History

The concept of a DAME has evolved over time as information technologies transformed the development of library automation, the creation of integrated content management systems, and the expansion of web-based discovery platforms. Overall, the evolving nature of the concept of a DAME can be traced to librarians, archivists, and museum curators' abilities to leverage the benefits of information technology with a particular focus on faster computing processing environments and retrieval speeds.[2] Additionally, over time, larger, more varied storage capacities also allowed GLAM institutions to achieve operational efficiencies to facilitate the large-scale digitization of distinctive analog collections as well as manage the exponential growth of born-digital materials, research data, and rich media. As changes emerged over the past sixty years, GLAM institutions saw a gradual shift in institutional missions that focused on access to in-house collections for their local patron base to raising the visibility of their collections to serve diverse transnational communities within a global information landscape.[3]

For academic libraries, the automation and streamlining of collection-management services was a critical factor in guiding this overall transformation. In the 1960s, academic libraries focused on streamlining acquisitions and cataloging workflows with the development of the first integrated library system (ILS). Library automation facilitated resource-sharing as well as the ability to augment bibliographic data and streamline core collection-management processes. As Christine Borgman writes, "the development of library automated systems can be seen as a gradual consolidation of programs and tools that each address a given area of the library's work into more . . . unified platforms resulting in streamlined and integrated workflows and processes" across institutions.[4]

In the 1980s, the creation and marketing of integrated library systems, the implementation of multiresource library databases, and the retroconversion of bibliographic data contributed to the shift from a *traditional library catalog* to an *online library system*. For many libraries, the ILS transformed the idea of providing access to material that was physically owned by a library to "a resource-sharing model" that provided a wide array of information resources via library consortia lending programs. "Integrated online resources" gave new meaning to identifying, locating, and obtaining descriptive metadata for archival and museum collections as well as other related primary source material that remained hidden and inaccessible to remote researchers.[5]

The shift from sharing highly structured, complex bibliographic records to linked digital or digitized content emerged in the 2010s with library services platforms (LSAs). As "a new product service genre," LSAs challenged the model of automation centered on print-based materials by offering "a cluster of ancillary products such as link resolvers, electronic resource management systems, digital asset management systems, and other repository systems" aimed to simplify library operations through "a more integrative platform" designed to handle different types of content.[6] As librarians were confronted with complex user needs and expectations, LSAs were considered a fundamental tool to interface with larger institutional systems and national and international networks of linked data and digital content. In addition, LSAs offered institutions not only the ability to virtually represent their collections in new ways, but also to search across digital holdings, which included distinctive collections, commercial databases, government sources, museum collections, and research data.[7] As the act of centralizing digital assets and associated metadata became situated at the center of managing, receiving, and granting access to information resources, librarians' and archivists' work has focused more and more on processing distinctive materials in a variety of digital formats made available by unified discovery platforms.[8]

While libraries integrated areas of collection-management operations for more effective and efficient processing of digital-information resources, archivists and records managers focused on what they referred to as the greatest challenge of the "digital age." In the late 1960s, the lifecycle management of electronic records laid the groundwork for early data curation and digital-preservation methodologies. Historically, many digital-preservation theories, principles, and conceptual models emanated with archivists' and records managers' challenge of mitigating data loss and maintaining long-term accessibility to electronic records in the face of media obsolescence, hardware and software failure, data degradation, human error, and an array of external threats. Primarily, early government archivists, who focused on large datasets stored on magnetic tapes generated by mainframe computers, felt the greatest urgency and risk for continuity of government services as a result of mass data loss due to corruption, degradation, and media obsolescence.[9]

Understanding that early intervention was the key to long-term accessibility of electronic records, archivists at the National Archives and Records Administration (NARA) adopted "upfront records management," an approach that was centered on intervening early within the lifecycle management of data to combat media and hardware obsolescence. NARA archivists also developed a continuum of digital preservation actions that occurred throughout the lifecycle management of electronic records. Grounded in traditional archival theory of provenance and record authenticity and integrity, archivists institutionalized file reformatting, system migration, emulation, and data normalization as preservation strategies for managing the federal government's early digital records.[10]

By the 1990s, government data scientists working for NASA led the initiative of data preservation and, within the Consultative Committee for Space Data Systems (CCSDS), developed the Open Archival Information System (OAIS) reference model as a high-level conceptual framework and a key standard for digital repository development. The OAIS model reflects the lifecycle management of digital assets ranging from ingest to storage and dissemination, outlines ongoing preservation actions and environmental monitoring, and underscores the importance of administrative and preservation planning. The OAIS reference model was first published as an ISO standard in 2003 and has undergone several iterations but remains the core model for digital preservation infrastructure development for GLAM institutions.[11]

With the establishment of the OAIS reference model as an international standard, the focus of digital preservation shifted from ad hoc institutional projects to include infrastructure as a major component in digital preservation plans and programs. In 2007, the Preservation and Reformatting Section (PARS) Working Group of the American Library Association (ALA) referred to the OAIS as the accepted standard and used the model to frame a new definition of digital preservation. This refined definition stated that digital preservation included a combination of "policies, strategies and actions to ensure accurate rendering of authenticated content overtime, regardless of the challenge of media failure and technological change." In the PARS plan, the long-term management, monitoring, and focus on digital content was just as important as the need for "active preservation" procedures and a corresponding information technology infrastructure that would serve to create a viable, secure, and sustainable preservation environment.[12]

Building on the OAIS model, the emergence of institutional repositories (IRs) and digital-asset management systems in the 2000s was also a major component of the history of DAME development as digital repositories combined key elements of the OAIS functional model, digital preservation, and open access. Throughout the 2000s, the evolving nature of IRs would ultimately alter e-scholarship and research data curation practices for most research institutions. Traditionally, scholarly communication had been based on the "self-contained nature" of books, journals, and conference proceedings as the key output of scholarship within IRs' publishing structures. As the nature and scale of research data changed, transformations also occurred within the scholarly communication landscape with the adoption of new data-mining tools and associated data-management services for locating, managing, analyzing, and visualizing research data output via open-access e-research platforms.[13]

Over the past ten years, institutional repositories have expanded to include broader digital-asset management functionality for the purpose of providing access to a range of digital content that extends beyond institutional publications to distinctive digital-collection building. Specifically, the desire to incorporate rich media production, use, and re-use into a range of broader public engagement and research processes has driven the demand for increased integration of DAME functions within an institution's information repository structure. As IRs morphed into enterprise digital repositories, the GLAM sector has welcomed the expansion of search functionalities to provide filtered and faceted retrieval capabilities, workflow development capabilities that facilitate the ingest, review, storage, and retrieval of assets, as well as the addition of metadata harvesting, capture, and exporting features. Some IRs include transcoding and migration tools that enable normalization and replication of multiple versions of the asset for access and preservation purposes, as well as custom application programming interfaces (APIs), which allow for uploading and downloading to the IR from websites. Increasingly, IRs and digital repositories have access-control lists and authentication tools that help facilitate permissions for various user groups as well as reporting functions that document holding metrics and auditing on all system actions.[14]

By the mid-2010s, basic DAME principles were increasingly being expressed by information and information system managers in libraries, museums, and archives as a type of master data management (MDM). Faced with the situation where departments and units across an organization were gathering the same information and holding it locally in inconsistent and incompatible formats, DAME principles were incorporated with a series of systems and tools that would enable uniformity in stewardship and accountability for a universe of digital assets managed by the same institution.[15]

GLAM institutions have long since recognized the incalculable benefits that open access, open source, and open standards confer, and modern-day DAME development is greatly influenced, designed, and managed with these concepts in mind. Although open access continues to be a central element in the expansion of IRs, the importance of managing these assets in a trustworthy digital preservation environment has emerged as an important component of e-research platforms and digital repositories as well. Future challenges are significant as GLAM institutions contemplate strategies relating to the integration of "big data," time-based media, and an acquisition model of "data as collections" into existing collection-management workflows.[16] In addition, data management plans have required GLAM institutions, which seek funding from public and private granting agencies, to articulate data-curation and digital-preservation philosophies and plans at the institutional and multi-institution level to ensure long-term open access to digital collections. In this context, the concept of a DAME continues to evolve to ensure the sustainability of new forms of digital assets accessed within more unified and integrated digital-asset platforms, which include research data as well as distinctive digital collections, open educational resources, artifacts, rich media, art work, institutional records, and licensed e-content.[17]

A Digital Stewardship Framework Defined

In the context of limited resources, DAME development emerged as GLAM institutions contemplated more holistic digital-preservation and digital-curation infrastructures to navigate enterprise challenges, and by way, have ushered in a "digital stewardship service model." This model encompasses enterprise strategies that serve to align acquisitions, metadata creation, data curation, and digital preservation through integrative collection management supported by a scalable digital infrastructure. This framework, which fosters collaborative approaches to content creation, access, and preservation, can be defined by the following principles:

1. *Digital stewardship begins by understanding the scope and scale of the digital-asset ecosystem.*

    In the age of information abundance, defining the scope and scale of a digital-asset ecosystem can be challenging. Within any ecosystem, digital assets can take many forms, including video, graphic images, photographs, textual documents, datasets, software, databases, published research, Computer-aided Design (CAD) drawings and Geographic Information Systems (GIS) data, time-based artwork, websites, email and social media, and open educational resources and digital-learning modules. While "digital content," "digital objects," "digital collections," "digital material," and "digital resources" are often used interchangeably, a shared understanding of the definition of "a digital asset" is essential in order to assess and develop cost-effective plans to manage the universe of data that is created, managed, and maintained by any library, archive, or museum.

    Although digital assets can mean different things to different people who work at different types of GLAM institutions, for the purposes of

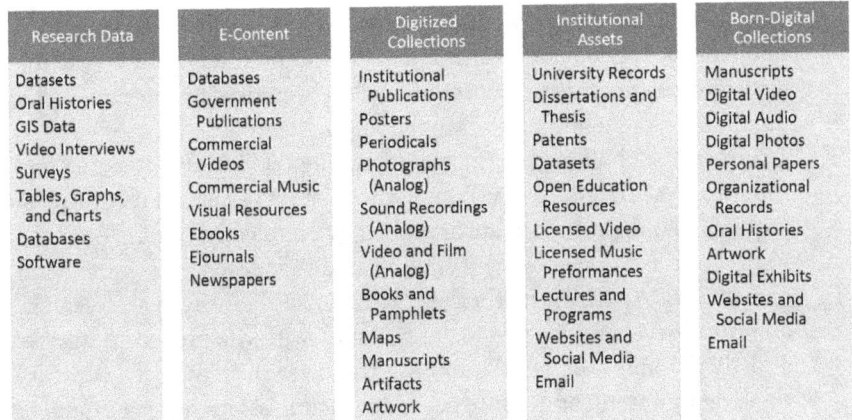

Figure 1.1. Understanding the Digital Asset Ecosystem

this book, a digital asset is defined as *"a unit of information"* that has significant properties and characteristics that must be maintained over time in order to remain accessible, usable, and meaningful.[18] The fundamental characteristics of any digital asset that must be maintained or preserved over time are referred to as "significant properties" which include:

- content
- context
- structure
- appearance
- function
- dynamism

All digital assets have specific, well-defined characteristics, functions, structures, content, and contexts which are conveyed through metadata.[19] Preserving the significant properties of any digital asset is the essence of good digital stewardship as it ensures that any asset's authenticity and integrity is retained over time. Trustworthy digital repositories that manage and store digital assets place a high degree of importance on data integrity and authenticity and incorporate a wide array of security and environmental controls to ensure the preservation of assets over time.[20] Given the specific, and often complex, nature of digital collections, active and systematic metadata management is essential in order to sustain a digital-asset ecosystem. In addition to metadata management, digital curatorial functions encompass a wide range of specialized actions, tools, and workflows that ensure that the associated characteristics, specifically the "significant properties," of a digital asset are maintained throughout its lifecycle.

Given the challenge of the exponential growth in data volume and file size, good digital stewardship, in the context of GLAM institutions, requires that digital assets are appraised by established criteria outlined in a collection-development policy and conveyed via submission agreements. Appraisal methodologies balance the historical, research, administrative, and legal value of the asset with the preservation risks and the overall cost of maintaining the asset over time. In addition to varied content and contexts, most digital assets have a complex structure and production process, which may include the creation of multiple derivatives or proxy files. For example, the production lifecycle of rich media may include digital production raw files, edited file versions, preservation and access masters, as well as a variety of versions of the final production copy and associated proxy files. Because production files can be large in size, multifaceted, and created in a wide variety of proprietary file formats, duplication and file redundancy of rich media assets pose a chronic challenge for curators, archivists, and librarians who often must ascertain the working or preproduction files from the official or final production copy of any digital asset.[21]

In addition to identifying the various versions of an asset, digital rights management is a critical component in assessing any ecosystem. For GLAM institutions, rights management may encompass a wide spectrum of assets that an institution owns or are licensed under specific contractual agreements or are managed by an institution on behalf of a rights holder. In other instances, the rights to some assets may be unknown. The obligation to maintain records detailing information about the ownership, chain of custody, and reproduction and intellectual rights is essential for the current and future use of any digital content. Aligning rights management with designated permissions for use and reuse is critical to protecting digital content as well as guiding informed decisions that shape the contours of legal and ethical stewardship that are unique to each institution.[22]

2. *Digital stewardship takes into consideration the totality of challenges associated with maintaining and sustaining digital assets over time.*

Much larger in scope than data curation, digital preservation, or information and knowledge management, the concept of digital stewardship provides a holistic framework for managing digital content at

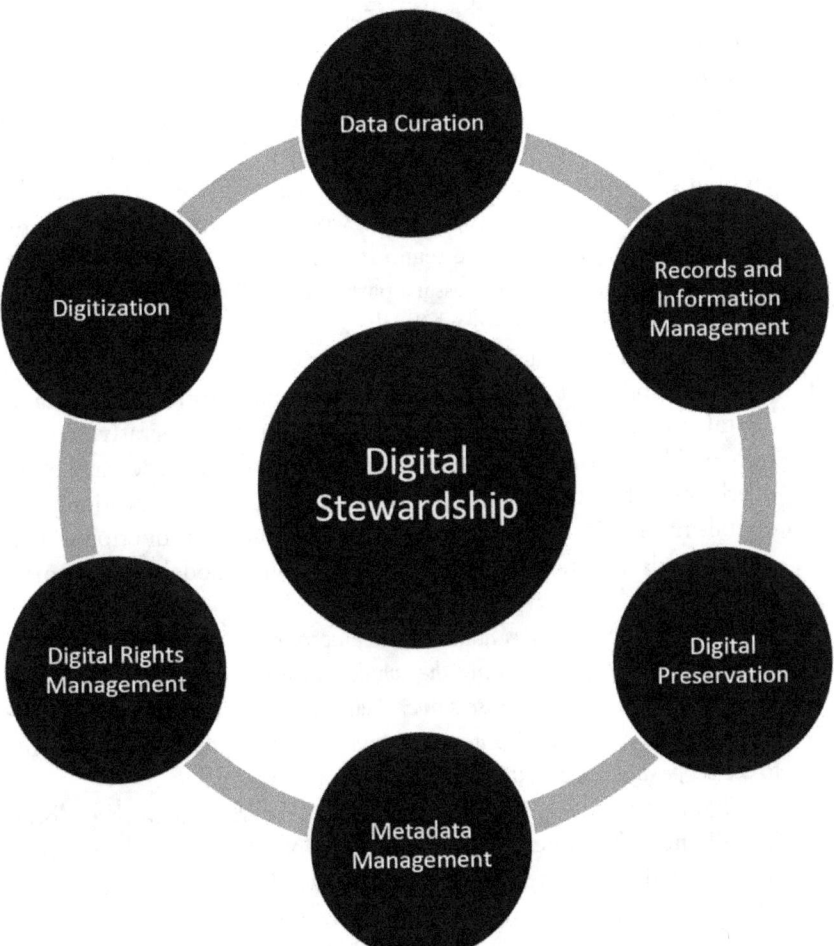

Figure 1.2. Digital Stewardship Activities

an enterprise level. Digital stewardship includes the entirety of processes relating to digital curation, digital preservation, and information and knowledge management—all of which emphasize the importance of added value, trusted information, and active management of digital content over time. Framing the management of digital content under the term digital stewardship provides a more holistic view of all the activities that need to be undertaken, including developing a digital strategy and a set of policies, tools, assessment techniques, workflows, and processes that ensure the preservation as well as the use and reuse of a range of digital assets over time.[23]

For most institutions, the lines between digital stewardship functions are not always distinct or clear cut, and functional gaps may exist for the critical steps needed for managing digital content. In some institutions, digital preservation is bounded by certain tasks with other activities under the umbrella of "digital curation" or "digital archiving," while for other institutions digital preservation may be aligned with IT or conceived as the work of an institutional strategist within an administrative team. It is important to note that, while digital preservation is a necessary part of digital stewardship, it is not enough by itself. Likewise, while the objective of digital curation is to produce and manage data in ways that ensure longevity, integrity, and accessibility, it does not often include administrative advocacy, digital strategy, and resource planning or focus on integrative collection building. Strategies for good digital stewardship encompass the overlapping functions of digital curation, digital preservation, and digital-information management that extend beyond functional definitions and, rather, encompass a holistic service model for the entire organization.[24]

3. *Digital stewardship implies administrative accountability, which is not only demonstrated by implementing the whole range of collection-management processes applied to digital assets over their life span but also through a commitment to resource development and financial sustainability commensurate to the scope and scale of the digital ecosystem.*

Digital stewardship is defined as the good care of data throughout its full lifecycle, which includes its creation through its reuse. The multifaceted components of digital stewardship include interconnected processes, cross-functional workflows, overarching policies, and conceptual models and philosophies that constitute the larger digital service model for an institution. Good stewardship is also an institutional investment that requires significant resource development and continual maintenance of curatorial and preservation environments that extend the life of any asset. In addition, resources may be required to enable greater discoverability and usability as well as to facilitate the virtual interrelatedness of assets.[25]

Good stewardship often begins by setting standards for lifecycle management that support "curation-ready" assets at the point of asset creation. It also focuses on "value-added" services like metadata creation, enhancement, and harvesting to ensure accessibility through diversified discovery platforms. With the exponential growth of digital collections, digital stewardship requires active management and systematic monitoring, as well as sustainable resources and infrastructure development to not only ensure preservation and accessibility but also to support the discovery and reuse of digital assets. Finally, digital stewardship implies administrative and financial accountability, which is demonstrated by an institutional commitment that is formalized through a mandate and budgetary dollars to ensure a sustainable information infrastructure and trained personnel to accomplish the work.[26]

4. *A foundational element of digital stewardship is developing a digital-asset management ecosystem (DAME) that stores and distributes digital assets in a controlled, uniform, and centrally managed infrastructure.*

    A DAME should facilitate the entire spectrum of digital stewardship activities, including ensuring long-term accessibility and reuse of digital content as well as managing risks associated with the health and security of an asset throughout its lifecycle. DAME development is reliant on collaboration, as it draws together digital practitioners with complementary skill sets in order to enrich, streamline, and consolidate the management of a vast array of digital content across the institution. This approach reduces the siloization of collection management and promotes digital-stewardship activities that can be undertaken early in the lifecycle of digital content.[27]

5. *Good digital stewardship is both a professional and a societal responsibility.*

    Finally, responsible digital stewardship considers a repository's realistic capacity to care for collections when deciding to acquire or deaccession digital assets. Underlying these activities are the greater social responsibilities for librarians, archivists, and curators who maintain the integrity and authenticity of digital assets in their care. Since GLAM institutions manage archival and cultural heritage collections that increase social awareness, serve as cultural memory, and contribute to the historical record, digital collections often serve the public good. As such, digital stewardship is rooted in "the ethics of care" that prioritizes trustworthy and sustainable practices and policies.[28]

Digital Stewardship: Roles and Responsibilities

For most GLAM institutions, good stewardship begins as early in the lifecycle as possible. Early intervention begins with engaging creators, data custodians, and users of digital content. Early lifecycle management may include working with data creators on the design of DAME systems, developing cogent comprehensive functional requirements for assessing new tools and software, creating policies relating to the acquisition of digital content, institutionalizing protocols for appropriate transfer, handling, and ingest of digital assets, as well as working with asset producers on approaches to content creation and management of associated metadata. Because digital stewardship is a shared responsibility that cuts across units, departments, and institutional lines, it should be guided by a high-level strategy that involves stakeholders from across the organization who will offer unique expertise and perspectives in order to promote cross-functional dialogue and collaboration.[29] Several kinds of stakeholders play important roles and are likely to have different perspectives on the various uses and significance of assets. Institutional stakeholders who may have a vested interest in digital stewardship may include:

- archivists
- chief information officers and IT staff
- project managers
- knowledge managers and data stewards
- metadata technical staff
- data librarians
- digital preservationists
- curators, registrars, and subject specialists
- records managers
- digital asset managers
- faculty, students, and scholars
- institutional stakeholders and donors

In addition to content specialists, digital stewardship requires the support of specialized technical practitioners, as well as administrators who can advocate for a substantial resource investment based on a digital strategy. This strategy should outline a business continuity plan that includes a discussion on return on investment (ROI), efficiencies and cost modeling, and a programmatic plan guided by a needs assessment and future cost projections that illustrate the urgency for investing in digital stewardship at an enterprise level.[30]

Information Governance and Digital Advocacy

For libraries, archives, and museums, there is a close correlation between digital stewardship and information governance (IG). Currently, most GLAM institutions lack sustainable digital stewardship services with governance business models that outline shared responsibilities to support the creation and management of digital assets at an enterprise level. Simply defined, IG encompasses how an organization manages the totality of its digital assets. With the unprecedented growth of digital assets, the diversity of file formats, and the importance of information security compliance, information governance is central in guiding the framework for the creation, accessibility, and preservation of digital assets across any enterprise or institutional partnership. IG includes the policies, processes, and workflows relating to the creation, organization, management, use, storage, and protection of digital assets. It establishes the contours of the rights and responsibilities of digital stewardship and therefore is ongoing and multifaceted. It also encompasses the continuous management of technological platforms and tools that emerge over time.[31] IG ensures institutional accountability with federal and state laws, institutional guidelines and policies, as well as compliance with legal frameworks specific to the institution. Finally, IG provides an integrated, centralized approach to decision-making relating to managing, processing, controlling, archiving, accessing, and securing digital content at an enterprise level.[32]

Since the boundaries of ownership for institutional assets are not always clear in GLAM institutions, IG requires at least one executive sponsor who understands the basic tenets of digital stewardship and can assist in advocacy and cross-functional collaborations with a variety of stakeholders. Oftentimes, IG policies institutionalize the work of specific "data stewards" who are guided by a "system of decisions points, responsibilities, rights, and accountabilities for information-related processes" that designate how data can be used, accessed, and stored.[33] For GLAM institutions, there should be a corresponding connection between IG, digital stewardship initiatives, and a governance mandate associated with institutional policies, a mission statement, and related strategic initiatives.

Approaches to garnering institutional support for digital stewardship and information governance include:

- appealing to the official charter or mission statement of the institution in order to advocate for digital stewardship priorities
- leveraging quantitative assessment in order to identify digital collections' strengths and risks
- building on successes by highlighting service points relating to the teaching, learning, and research mission of the institution and constituent base

- leveraging a records-management mandate that includes a legal responsibility to identify and preserve records of enduring historical, administrative, and legal value
- improving efficiencies in complying with Freedom of Information (FOIA) requests and e-discovery compliance
- recognizing data management as a core service for grant and gift stewardship
- making the correlation between the proliferation of born-digital assets and a return on investment and cost savings over time

Strategic alignment with the vision of the institution as well as solidifying the support of an enterprise-level executive sponsor help to build awareness and advocate for necessary resources for the future. In addition, building "an advocacy network" is fundamental to underscore issues of sustainable expansion of digital-stewardship initiatives over time. The centralization of digital assets offers budget savings and facilitates the delivery of assets to a variety of discovery and access platforms in order to enhance public engagement.

As GLAM institutions expand their mission as sites of innovation and invention, the ROI of safeguarding intellectual property rights and digital-rights management can only be realized through a collaborative digital-stewardship framework that celebrates and defines institutional identity and core values.[34] Additional talking points for making the case for institutional support for digital stewardship as an investment for the future may include:

- risk of information lost
- safeguarding history and protecting cultural heritage
- disruption of business continuity
- cost-effectiveness of early intervention
- risk of legal liability and compliance with federal and state legislation and institutional policies and guidelines
- increased accessibility and the power of discovery in supporting research, teaching, and public engagement
- enhance information security
- commitment to open data and open access
- centralization of rights information
- importance of connecting people to knowledge
- enhanced access and discovery

In addition, it is important to identify champions within an organization whose work is closely tied to digital stewardship, including the office of general counsel, the office of information technology, universities and research institutes, local businesses, and professional organizations. For libraries, archives, and museums, digital stewardship is mission-driven but should also be framed by necessity and urgency to act to preserve cultural heritage, social memory, and institutional history.[35]

Finally, garnering support for digital stewardship outside of the organization is a good way to expand an advocacy network as well as to extend the reach and impact of any organization. Public support can help leverage the significance of digital assets and expand global connections in a new era of data-driven scholarship that is interdisciplinary and transnational in nature. Given the social and cultural impact of the ever-expanding digital world, it is easy to make the case that digital stewardship, broadly defined, is a critical investment that ensures the use and reuse, integrity, authenticity, and trustworthiness of knowledge for future generations.

Notes

1. Robin R. Sewell et al., "When a Repository Is Not Enough: Redesigning a Digital Ecosystem to Serve Scholarly Communication," *Journal of Librarianship and Scholarly Communication*, 7 (2019): 3; Elizabeth Ferguson Keathley, *Digital Asset Management: Content Architectures, Project Management, and Creating Order Out of Media Chaos* (Berkeley, CA: Apress, 2014), 4.

2. Joe Matthews, "A Nostalgic Look Back at Library Hi Tech(nology)," *Library Hi Tech*, 35, no. 1 (March 20, 2017): 94.

3. Christine Borgman, "From Acting Locally to Thinking Globally: A Brief History of Library Automation," *Library Quarterly* 67, no. 3 (July 1, 1997): 216–17.

4. Ibid., 222–23.

5. Ibid.

6. Marshall Breeding, "Introductions and Concepts," *Library Technology Reports* 51, no. 4 (2015): 6.

7. Ibid., 7.

8. Keathley, *Digital Asset Management*, 14.

9. Angela Fritz, "'So Many Options, So Little Time': How to Evaluate a Digital Preservation System That is Right for Your Institution," in *Digital Preservation in Libraries: Preparing for a Sustainable Future*, eds. Jeremy Myntti and Jessalyn Zoom (Chicago: American Library Association, 2019), 78.

10. Patricia C. Franks, *Records and Information Management* (Chicago: American Library Association, 2013), 5–11.

11. Edward M. Corrado and Heather Moulaison Sandy, *Digital Preservation for Libraries, Archives, and Museums* (Lanham, MD: Rowman & Littlefield, 2017), 54–55.

12. "Definitions of Digital Preservation: Prepared by the ALCTS Preservation and Reformatting Section, Working Group on Defining Digital Preservation," accessed October 25, 2019, http://www.ala.org/alcts/resources/preserv/2009def.

13. Gillian Oliver and Ross Harvey, *Digital Curation* (Chicago: Neal-Schuman, 2016), 22–23.

14. Marianne Buehler, *Demystifying the Institutional Repository for Success* (Oxford, England: Chandos Publishing, 2014), 1–28.

15. Katharine Schopflin, "Information Management Approaches to Digital Asset Management: A Case Study in Success and Failure," *Journal of Digital Media Management*, vol. 3-4 (2015): 309–19.

16. Thomas Padilla, "On a Collections as Data Imperative," February 15, 2017, accessed October 29, 2019, retrieved from UC Santa Barbara, https://escholarship.org/uc/item/9881c8sv.

17. Sewell et al., "When a Repository Is Not Enough," 3; Buehler, *Demystifying the Institutional Repository for Success*, 11.

18. Richard Peace-Moses, "What Is a Digital Asset," *Persistence of Memory: Stewardship of Digital Assets*, paper presented at NEDCC Conference, November 2005, http://www.pearcemoses.info/papers/NEDCC_DigitalAsset_2006.pdf.

19. Laura Krier and Carly Strasser, *Data Management for Libraries* (Chicago: American Library Association, 2014), 53–54.

20. Oliver and Harvey, *Digital Curation*, 118–19.

21. Anthony Cocciolo, *Moving Image and Sound Collections for Archivists* (Chicago: Society of American Archivists, 2017), 51–65.

22. Corrado and Sandy, *Digital Preservation for Libraries*, 37.

23. Somaya Langley, "Digital Preservation Should be More Holistic: A Digital Stewardship Approach," in *Digital Preservation in Libraries: Preparing for a Sustainable Future*, eds. Jeremy Myntti and Jessalyn Zoom (Chicago: American Library Association), 96–97.

24. Jaime McCurry, "Digital Stewardship: The One with All the Definitions," *The Collation* (blog), accessed October 25, 2019, https://collation.folger.edu/2014/04/digital-stewardship-the-one-with-all-the-definitions/; Butch Lazorchak, "Digital Preservation, Digital Curation, Digital Stewardship: What's in (Some) Names?" *The Signal* (blog), accessed October 25, 2019, https://blogs.loc.gov/thesignal/2011/08/digital-preservation-digital-curation-digital-stewardship-what%E2%80%99s-in-some-names/.

25. Ibid.

26. Lazorchak, "Digital Preservation, Digital Curation, Digital Stewardship."

27. Langley, "Digital Preservation Should be More Holistic," 104–105.

28. See SAA Core Value Statement and Code of Ethics, accessed October 25, 2019, https://www2.archivists.org/statements/saa-core-values-statement-and-code-of-ethics.

29. Oliver and Harvey, *Digital Curation*, 58–61.

30. Keathley, *Digital Asset Management*, 4.

31. Robert Smallwood, *Information Governance: Concepts, Strategies, and Best Practices* (Hoboken, NJ: Wiley, 2014), 5–6.

32. Franks, *Records and Information Management*, 29.

33. Stacy Kowalczyk, *Digital Curation for Libraries and Archives* (Santa Barbara, CA: Libraries Unlimited, 2018), 77.

34. Keathley, *Digital Asset Management*, 2, 16.

35. Trevor Owens, *The Theory and Craft of Digital Preservation* (Baltimore, MD: Johns Hopkins University, 2018), 9–10.

CHAPTER TWO

Assessing the Digital Asset Management Ecosystem

A Holistic Approach

A digital-stewardship assessment provides a holistic overview that can bridge the awareness of an institution's current technical infrastructure with the strengths of its digital collections, as well as the technological gaps that need to be filled to support future growth of the larger DAME. An essential first step in conceptualizing a digital-stewardship framework for any GLAM institution is assessing the scope and scale of the digital-asset ecosystem, including the varying subject content, the differing formats, and the ranges in file sizes and the total volume of digital content. In this context, assessment is defined as a comprehensive evaluation of an organization's ability to care for and preserve the entirety of its digital holdings. The goal of a digital-stewardship assessment is to identify "the current state" and scope of the digital-asset ecosystem, as well as the anticipated needs, in order to lay the groundwork for unified approaches to managing the growth of digital assets in the future. Essential to this process is surveying the use, access, and preservation needs of the collection in order to articulate the impact of the existing conditions, environment, policies, and infrastructure on digital assets at an enterprise level. In addition, a holistic needs assessment evaluates resources, policies, personnel, and technology in order to develop a digital-stewardship strategy that will meet the future needs of the entire institution.[1]

For GLAM institutions, digital stewardship assessment has often been hampered by the diverse quantity of digital content that is managed on different platforms, in separate systems, in disparate storage locations, and by redundant stewardship processes. Holistic digital-stewardship assessment is the first step in developing a defined digital strategy and framework that is oriented toward reducing the siloization and redundancy of institutional workflows. Moving beyond the unit-based approach, a holistic digital-stewardship assessment departs from a sole subject, format, or specific unit and looks across the organization by analyzing collections, stewardship practices and workflows, information systems, and collection-management policies. Holistic assessment provides essential data that will shape collection-management approaches across the organization and ultimately inform the digital strategy or future roadmap for the institution.[2]

A Multiple-Method Approach

Many organizations have attempted to initiate a digital-stewardship assessment by developing piecemeal survey strategies and methodologies that have been designed specifically for the needs of a single department or unit. In contrast to this approach, holistic assessment provides an overview of an institution's digital ecosystem and acknowledges the interconnected and interdependent nature of digital assets and information systems that are managed by a single organization. Holistic assessment takes a wide perspective using a multiple-method and multilevel approach to building a comprehensive and in-depth snapshot of digital assets at the enterprise level. The use of multiple datasets, methodologies, and tools enables this assessment approach to be flexible to the unique needs of the institution. The advantages of this multicomponent approach are the abilities to build an adaptable framework for immediate needs, as well as to incorporate long-term goals based on a technology plan that outlines not only what should be done but also how prioritized recommendations can be implemented. Most importantly, a holistic stewardship assessment drives technology selection and implementation that is aligned with the unique contours of the digital-asset ecosystem for the institution.[3]

At a high-level, a digital-stewardship assessment provides a range of long-term benefits. An assessment enables an institution to understand the totality of the ecosystem while identifying high-impact areas for resource development. By outlining strengths, weaknesses, challenges, and opportunities for growth, a digital-stewardship assessment supports evidence-based decisions in order to advocate and communicate with institutional stakeholders regarding the long-term investment and evolving nature of digital policies, services, and operations. Assessment helps make the case for digital stewardship by illustrating the scope and scale of digital collections in order to demonstrate the expanded roles and responsibilities that are necessary for new digital service programmatic areas. For many GLAM institutions, a digital-stewardship assessment is key to aligning optimal approaches for collection care and management, budget allocation needs, and the justification for expanding digital services in strategically targeted areas.[4] For institutions who have a goal of building digital capacities and capabilities, digital-stewardship assessment fosters a comprehensive understanding of the complexity, scale, and scope of digital collections; provides an awareness for existing and new staff and faculty to these challenges; and establishes critical benchmarks for future evaluations of digital-asset initiatives, resource levels, and professional development plans.[5]

In addition, a digital-stewardship assessment should set the context for an institution's technology strategy by outlining the need for an infrastructure that is scalable with integrated support to sustain the digital-asset management ecosystem over time. A digital-stewardship assessment lays the foundation for future system decisions relating to upgrading and migrating to new platforms and also provides an opportunity to reexamine infrastructure decisions and storage options.[6] With the goal of integrated collection building in mind, assessment outlines how the complex network of software and application programming interfaces (APIs) work together to centralize the creation, maintenance, and preservation of digital assets across the institution. Holistic evaluation of the technological infrastructure can shed light on a host of "special needs" relating to digital-asset management practices; storage and security environments; antiquated hardware, software, and information systems; the range of sensitive and confidential information; and the scope of digital rights management. As the basis for a technology plan, a digital-stewardship assessment is at the heart of continuous improvement, as it establishes a roadmap that encourages proactive evaluation as well as a cycle of active management and technical realignment as an ongoing process.[7]

Libraries, archives, and museums may apply multiple tools and matrices as part of a holistic assessment approach that pulls together a variety of quantitative and qualitative data and internal and external measures to assess the complexity of the digital-asset ecosystem. In addition to multiple-methods, holistic assessment addresses strategic and practical elements of collection care and overall management as it encompasses interviews with staff from across the institution, including collection development staff and IT specialists as well as members of curatorial and technical services. This cross-functional approach to assessment reflects wider perspectives that may reveal special characteristics of digital collections that are unique to an institution with the goal of identifying ways to create more agile staffing, responsive workflows, and appropriate resources for enterprise level digital-asset management.[8]

Digital-Stewardship Assessment Segmentation

Given the exponential growth of digital content, digital-stewardship assessment can be overwhelming, especially for organizations with limited resources. In order to lay the groundwork for building an enterprise digital strategy, holistic assessment can be broken down into components or manageable parts. "Assessment segmentation" is a useful framework for an enterprise approach that requires survey efforts to be broken down into phases or logical parts of the DAME.[9] Each segment enumerates digital assets from a broad to narrow continuum, which is comprised of four distinct levels that deconstruct the assessment into smaller, step-by-step pieces.[10] Organized from a high-level scan to a more granular evaluation, the levels of holistic digital-stewardship assessment may include an internal environmental

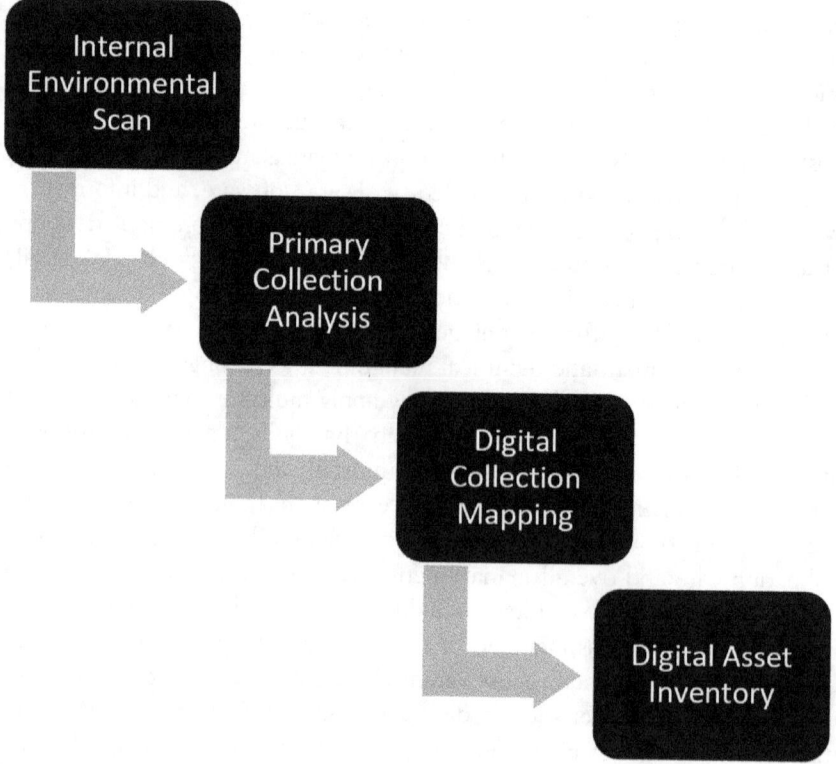

Figure 2.1. **Four Levels of Digital-Stewardship Assessment**

scan, a primary digital analysis, digital-collection mapping, and digital-asset inventories.

The internal environmental scan generally focuses on institutional capacity by examining the organization's policies and governance structures, including its leadership and management, overall staffing, and budgetary allocation.[11] An internal environmental scan begins by analyzing the organizational structure, the functional roles of programs, divisions, and units as well as general policies, business processes, and high-level workflows. In addition, an internal environmental scan includes an overview of existing information technology, tools, software, systems, and platforms.[12] An important component of an internal scan is analyzing the personnel assigned to activities relating to digital-asset management with a special focus on knowledge and skill level, as well as percentage of time and capacity that staff members devote to digital stewardship. An approach to conceptualizing the larger ecosystem may include analyzing the organizational chart and leadership models to begin to map potential collaborations and cross-functional workflows across the institution.[13] Stakeholder interviews are an important component of an internal environmental scan as well. Interviews can assist in identifying "pain points" or challenges relating to digital-content management . . . specific technology needs . . . resource requirements, and the acquisition, distribution, access, and discovery paths for assets.

While the internal environmental scan serves as background information, the primary digital analysis represents the composition of a large, complex ecosystem from a bird's-eye view. The primary analysis is not an inventory of every format of every asset, but it should indicate the range of digital assets, who manages the assets, and how they are used. The primary analysis facilitates high-level identification of assets, charts data sources, formats, and size, as well as identifies current workflows. Representing a high-level assessment of the ecosystem, the primary analysis categorizes born-digital and digitized assets found across the institution into broad categories, which can be presented in a graphic visualization. While any of the categories within the digital analysis can incorporate many types of files, formats, rendering software, relationships, and metadata, the analysis is meant to provide a springboard for conversation and a logical starting point for discussing stewardship in terms of identifiable groupings, organized around digital content, formats, or functional workflows.[14] A graphic depiction of the record types and infrastructure, as well as the operational and storage environments should also be included in the primary analysis, which will aid later with collection mapping and the digital-asset inventory process.[15]

With the primary analysis as a guide, collection mapping allows institutions to delve into a deeper level of assessment by charting the consistency of digital-asset management across the institution. Along with the primary analysis, collection mapping can identify specific needs, challenges, commonalities, and strengths relative to each collection. While digital collections may need different assessment procedures and approaches, collection mapping can help communicate the scope of the ecosystem with an eye toward specific policy needs. Collection analysis can also help unearth redundancies, as well as identify areas of overlap and gaps in workflows, information systems, and resources.

Building on the primary analysis, collection mapping evaluates digital assets based on their location, their subject content, and their specialized formats in order to assess short- and long-term stewardship needs. Most often, collection mapping focuses on "logical collections" grouped by subject, function, custodian, or record creator. Mapping indicates the relationships between collections, institutional departments, and components of information systems. More specifically, collection mapping includes an analysis of record creators and users and outlines the connection between those that manage digital content and the information systems that create, host, preserve, store, and provide access to digital assets. Mapping may also provide a total information systems overview known as "a data or collections atlas" with a complete list of information systems, storage locations, and functional areas of the institution with correlated stewardship functions.[16] Collection mapping may also be used to gauge areas of collection growth that may lead to recommendations for programmatic changes, targeted resource needs, or support for the creation of new workflows or services.[17]

At the most granular level, inventories quantify digital assets for current and future cost modeling and budgetary estimates. A digital-asset inventory is a detailed listing that includes the subject content, format types, replication copies, storage locations, dates, and file size for each asset.[18] The goal of an inventory is to quantify digital assets, while at the same time documenting the connections to associated collections as well as the overall primary analysis. Most often, inventories start with surveying material through technical appraisal to ascertain:

- organization of files through directory structures
- file size
- file format
- storage location
- creator, title, date, and description of content

- software, hardware, and operating system used to manage the asset
- rights, permissions, and access restrictions for each asset

These inventories should also include digital content that resides on legacy carriers such as floppy disks, hard drives, CD-ROMs, DVDs, and flash drives. Reported as "legacy content," inventories should differentiate born-digital assets from digitized collections.[19] Inventories should identify sensitive information, personally identifiable information (PII), terms of use and permissions, as well as assess the quality and appropriateness of associated metadata. Since inventories reveal the essential characteristics of each asset, granular assessment is critical in identifying and prioritizing care for high-value or high-risk assets as well as quantifying overall needs for the development of cross-functional workflows with a focus on functional gaps that currently exist in the institution.[20]

Assessment Models and Matrices

With multiple levels of the survey completed, digital-stewardship assessment turns to data analysis with a focus on identifying practical ways to raise operational readiness and build a prioritized recommendation list within the context of reasonable resource levels. Once the data is gathered, there are numerous frameworks and standards for evaluating digital stewardship assessment data. The following frameworks, models, and assessment tools may be helpful in data analysis and interpretation:

- **The Open Archival Information System (OAIS) Reference Model** is a conceptual framework for any digital archives system or repository that is dedicated to managing and preserving access to digital assets over the long term. The OAIS reference model outlines the stages of the digital-archive lifecycle in the context of a functional framework that presents the main components and basic data workflows within a digital preservation environment. The OAIS model also describes roles and responsibilities, defines designated user communities, and synthesizes the most essential digital stewardship activities, which cover ingest, preservation planning, archival storage, data management, administration, and access.[21]
- **The Trustworthy Repositories Audit and Certification Criteria and Checklist (TRAC) (ISO 16363 and 14721)** is based on the OAIS reference model and provides a pathway to establish a recognized trustworthy digital repository through a checklist of audit and certification

criteria. The checklist focuses on a digital repository's capability of reliably storing, migrating, and providing access to digital assets. TRAC facilitates assessment with an in-depth checklist of over one hundred requirements or criteria used by certified external auditors to measure trusted digital repositories. Both OAIS and TRAC serve as a foundation for sound stewardship practices by outlining standards-based criteria to support DAME development while focusing on organizational infrastructure, digital-object management, and technical infrastructure and security.[22]

- As a model to ascertain institutional readiness, the five stages of **the DPM Maturity Model** include acknowledge, act, consolidate, institutionalize, and externalize. Conceptualized at a high-level, this framework relates to not only the technologies in use but also the skills and resources needed to implement and develop a sustainable infrastructure, workflows, and policies for a wide-ranging approach to digital stewardship. This model can be helpful in communicating basic elements of a service model to upper administrators who have little to no knowledge of the technical or operational resources needed for sustainable stewardship programs.

- **The Digital Curation Centre's (DCC) Data Curation Lifecycle Model** represents core digital preservation and curation activities through a model of sequential lifecycle actions that range from ingest to appraisal to storage. The model is best used for building capacity and skill sets relating to research data management, as it maps out the stages of data curation and preservation throughout the research process. It is useful in identifying gaps in current practices, ensuring the documentation of policies and procedures, and helping refine strategies for future development.[23]

- **The National Digital Stewardship Alliance's (NDSA) Levels of Preservation** is a matrix that addresses storage and geographic location, file fixity and data integrity, information security, metadata, and file formats along four spectrums. Preservation levels are based on preservation actions in the following areas: data protection, data assessment, data monitoring, and data repair. The NDSA's levels of preservation are critical for assessing the "operational readiness" of any institution contemplating the implementation of a digital stewardship strategy and in managing a cost-effective storage plan. The NDSA Levels of Preservation Assessment Group has provided an assessment tool intended to offer baseline scoring on five functional complementary components including storage, integrity, control, metadata, and content. Self-scoring allows institutions to set goals, allocate resources, and advocate for digital stewardship among stakeholders and partners.[24]

- **The Digital Preservation Capacity Maturity Model (DPCMM)** includes fifteen areas of performance, each of which derive from the OAIS requirements. The model is organized around a series of baseline activities used to measure performance in specific areas of digital stewardship. The model assesses the following fourteen components: policy, strategy, governance, collaboration, technical expertise, open source/neutral formats, designated community, ingest, storage, device/media renewal, integrity, security, metadata, and access. DPCMM provides a score that ranges from one to five for each component, which allows institutions to focus on areas of digital stewardship that best fit their unique needs and resources.[25]

- **The CoreTrustSeal** replaced the Data Seal of Approval (DSA) and includes a self-assessment of sixteen guidelines. The framework is most often used for the implementation, verification, and standardization of the creation, storage, and use of research data. The requirements reflect core characteristics of trustworthy data repositories and are the culmination of cooperative efforts to harmonize data repository certification.[26]

- **The Digital Preservation Coalition Rapid Assessment Model (DPC-RAM)** is a digital preservation maturity modeling tool that has been designed to enable rapid benchmarking of an organization's digital stewardship capabilities. The DPC-RAM offers a straightforward assessment bullet list for several "criteria levels" rather than a deep-dive assessment closely associated with comprehensive certification tools. Areas of assessment cover organizational viability, policy and strategy, legal basis, IT capability, continuous improvement, and community. Service capacities include acquisition, transfer, ingest, bitstream preservation, content preservation, metadata management, and discovery and access.[27]

- **The Digital Repository Audit Method Based in Risk Assessment (DRAMBORA)** is a self-audit process that measures institutional risk. The toolkit was developed by the Digital Curation Centre (DCC) and Digital Preservation Europe (DPE) to identify, assess, and manage assets by coherently mapping critical preservation risks to the range of resources, activities, and drivers that characterize an institution's digital stewardship efforts.[28]

Risk-Management Assessment

Broad principles of risk management have been a longstanding practice for informing digital stewardship, because the active management of risk is essential to preserve digital objects and to ensure their usability in the future.[29] As a result, digital-stewardship assessment should address how well an institution:

- integrates digital preservation initiatives at the point of data creation
- uses open and well-documented standards and systems
- documents well-informed decisions
- uses nationally accepted metadata schemas
- documents an exit strategy for existing information systems, software, and storage providers, including a migration plan
- documents a plan for the decommission and succession of information systems[30]

A digital-stewardship assessment report may include a risk profile, which assists institutional stakeholders in understanding the implications associated with the mismanagement of digital assets. With a structured evaluative approach, a risk profile may even include a ranked top-ten list of greatest risks to digital assets, which may demonstrate the cost of inaction to institutional stakeholders.[31]

Unstructured Data, Total Cost of Ownership, and Cost Modeling

One of the most beneficial elements of a digital-stewardship assessment is an analysis of the scope and scale of unstructured data that exists within an ecosystem. Decentralized information systems and unstructured data pose some of the greatest obstacles for assessment, as the data may not have a metadata schema and may not be part of a database or have a formal directory structure. Unstructured data, across the enterprise, may reside on shared network drives, in legacy content archives, and in large caches of digital media. Unstructured data may live on personal computers and external storage devices, on laptops and tablets, within a Google suite, on PC hard drives, within third-party systems, and within cloud-service providers. The challenges of unstructured data are exacerbated by rapid technology obsolescence resulting in the inaccessibility of born-digital assets that reside on media carriers ranging from DVDs to hard drives to flash drives.[32] Digital and social media represents another area of exponential growth of unstructured data with its own associated costs relating to scale, size of data files, redundancy, and lack of consistent metadata to aid in search and discovery.

The cost of managing unstructured data should be addressed as part of any final assessment report. Archivists and records managers have long recognized the total cost of ownership (TCO) for managing and preserving unstructured data as a reoccurring financial commitment that encompasses indirect and direct costs relating to historical and technical appraisal, metadata remediation, PII review, deduplication, bit-level preservation, and storage costs. In assessing the digital-asset ecosystem, TCO can serve as a beneficial framework that illustrates the continuity and long-term maintenance of data as a perpetual cost that can be reduced and effectively managed by a digital-stewardship service model with a centralized infrastructure and a unified storage strategy at the enterprise level.[33]

In this sense, digital-stewardship assessment offers a unique opportunity to model the costs associated with the lifecycle of digital content. In stark contrast to analog and print-based collections, digital assets have ongoing infrastructure and storage costs, which are often reevaluated on a three- to five-year cycle and include associated costs for upgrades as well as the ongoing costs of reengineering infrastructures.[34] Additional organizational variables for digital-stewardship cost modeling include:

- the capacity of the organization (leadership, equipment, knowledge, and skills)
- the organization's tolerance for risk
- the existing volume of assets calculated in total file number and asset size
- the total cost for data migration and normalization over the course of lifecycle management
- the anticipated growth and speed at which data is created or acquired
- the current storage capacities and future needs of the organization
- the specific access requirements that impact network speeds
- the scope and sophistication of the existing technical infrastructure
- the need for advanced staff training and funding for new positions

A further complicating factor to cost modeling for digital-stewardship initiatives relates to evolving cloud-storage services, which are often an additional ongoing cost that must be drawn from an existing operational budget. In an era of shrinking budgets, digital stewardship activities may suddenly appear to cost an organization more, even though the long-term curatorial activities might be more cost-effective.[35] Although an assessment may illustrate the cost savings that occur with the centralization of a DAME, the analysis may also recommend revenue incentives to offset the future cost of digital stewardship at the enterprise level. Possible revenue streams may include:

- digital preservation-related endowments
- fees for services including storage, software, and consultations
- digitization on demand services
- access on demand services
- subscription, licensing, and reproduction fees
- acquisition budget integration
- centralizing stewardship cost as a result of a legal requirement or institutional mandate

Analysis and Prioritized Recommendations

An assessment report should offer a set of economically feasible recommendations to support the development of a reliable and sustainable digital-stewardship strategy.[36] Based on the goals of the digital-stewardship assessment, the analysis may include an evaluation of high-value, high-risk digital content based on the collection mapping and asset inventories. In addition, a file format analysis may determine the overlap and gaps between preferred, acceptable, unacceptable, and unknown (or not implemented) formats, which make up the entirety of the ecosystem. This analysis helps the institution develop a strategy based on implementing levels of preservation to address an estimated percentage of file formats that are at higher risk of degradation or obsolescence. Finally, the analysis should include an overview of information systems, tools, and software in use, with a specific focus on their functionality, as well as how existing and recommended tools fit into digital stewardship initiatives.[37]

Content and format analysis serve as a roadmap to guide institutional priorities for actions as well as outline a plan to respond to immediate challenges and needs of the ecosystem. A priority list may be based on the value of specific assets, the ease of workflow implementation, or the expense of assets that require the most extensive investment. Collection or format prioritization may include assessing the needs of the collection as a whole, at the level of use or anticipated use, or based on the uniqueness of digital content.[38] Finally, digital-asset prioritization should outline immediate digital stewardship tasks that can be implemented, as well as inform future acquisition decisions on the basis of long-term preservation requirements and associated costs. With the scope and scale of the current ecosystem in mind, the assessment can lend credence to carefully weigh the value of future digital acquisitions against the cost of storage, the current state of the assets, the viability of the formats, the overall size of the collection, and its potential for use and reuse.[39]

Assessment Report

It's important to keep in mind that the final digital-stewardship assessment report will be of interest to various institutional stakeholders and should include an explanation of methodology and practice, a summary of data, associated recommendations, the outline of a preliminary plan of action, a prioritization list with a timeline, and a cost projection and recommended cost model. Framed by the institutional mission and organizational initiatives, the final report offers clear objectives and goals, articulates the scope, and outlines recommendations of the assessment that are tailored to the realities of a given institution, its staffing levels, and budget constraints. The report should provide a holistic overview of the organization in order to understand the larger ecosystem, and outline the interrelated nature of the risks to digital assets based on how the different categories and levels of assessment interact with one another. The assessment should be understood in the context of a given institution and its distinctive collections in order to provide meaningful guidance that can be impactful and implemented successfully.[40]

In order to guide the institution, the plan, outlined in a final assessment report, should provide short-, medium-, and long-term recommendations that an organization can take to improve digital stewardship. It should offer practical ways to build operational readiness and articulate the scale of the infrastructure needed to manage and sustain an ecosystem that ensures the health and long-term accessibility of the entirety of digital assets within an institution's holdings. Finally, the assessment report should sketch out a plan of action to address the identified risks, as well as an associated list of prioritizations to indicate the level of importance for each action. Special considerations should be given to permission rights and access requirements, the quality of metadata, and the size of assets and related format types. The assessment analysis lays the groundwork for what is to follow in terms of resource development, as well as future approaches relating to collection management, appraisal methodologies, workflows for accessioning and processing, digital forensics, and digital preservation best practices including format specifications and normalization guidelines.[41]

Sharing the assessment report broadly with members of the organization is critical for digital-stewardship team-building. In these efforts, a communication plan may be helpful in framing conversations about the assessment report with clear goals, objectives, and recommendations. The assessment should acknowledge necessary collaborations with all levels of the organization in order to mitigate fears of organizational change and allay any concerns regarding future roles and work processes.[42] Framing assessment as an iterative, continuous process is important in managing staff expectations, in the context of changes in information technology, as well as evolving tools, techniques, and approaches. Finally, as the ultimate collaborative endeavor, digital stewardship requires periodic self-assessment and an openness for internal feedback. Internal surveys, peer review, and external auditing can measure work-related implications, and offer an outlet for suggesting improvements, as well as acknowledging future challenges.[43]

Notes

1. Madeline Kelly and Stephanie Smith, "Assessing Collections Holistically: A Behind-the-Scenes Approach," in *Assessment Strategies in Technical Services*, eds. Kimberley Edwards and Michelle Leonard (Chicago: American Library Association, 2019), 25.

2. Ibid.

3. Ibid., 30–31.

4. Madeline Kelly, "Applying the Tiers of Assessment: A Holistic and Systematic Approach to Assessing Library Collections," *The Journal of Academic Librarianship* 40, no. 6 (2014): 585.

5. Kelly and Smith, "Assessing Collections Holistically," 27.

6. Marilyn N. Ochoa, Laurie Taylor, and Mark Sullivan, *Digital Collections Assessment and Outreach*, SPEC Kit 341 (Washington, DC: Association of Research Libraries, August 2014), 14–15.

7. Charles Dollar and Lori Ashley, "Digital Preservation Capability Maturity Model: Background and Performance Metrics," May 16, 2014, accessed on February 10, 2020, https://static.squarespace.com/static/52ebbb45e4b06f07f8bb62bd/t/53765058e4b0d45559654406/1400262744481/2014%20May_DPCMM%20Background%20and%20Performance%20Metrics.pdfDigital%20Preservation%20Maturity%20Model.

8. Ibid., 25, 29.

9. Robert Smallwood, *Information Governance: Concepts, Strategies, and Best Practices* (Hoboken, NJ: Wiley, 2014), 156–57.

10. Kelly, "Applying the Tiers of Assessment," 586.

11. Stacy Kowalczyk, *Digital Curation for Libraries and Archives* (Santa Barbara, CA: Libraries Unlimited, 2018), 157.

12. Edward M. Corrado and Heather Moulaison Sandy, *Digital Preservation for Libraries, Archives, and Museums* (Lanham, MD: Rowman & Littlefield, 2017), 124.
13. Erin Baucom, "Planning and Implementing a Sustainable Digital Preservation Program," *Library Technology Reports* 55, no. 6 (Chicago: American Library Association, 2019), 13–14.
14. Kowalczyk, *Digital Curation for Libraries and Archives*, 164.
15. Smallwood, *Information Governance*, 160.
16. Patricia C. Franks, *Records and Information Management* (Chicago: American Library Association, 2013), 91.
17. Fletcher Durant, "Preservation Assessments," in *Assessment Strategies in Technical Services*, eds. Kimberley Edwards and Michelle Leonard (Chicago: American Library Association, 2019), 197.
18. Franks, *Records and Information Management*, 86.
19. Corrado and Sandy, *Digital Preservation for Libraries*, 239.
20. Durant, "Preservation Assessments," 184.
21. "The Open Archival Information System (OAIS) Reference Model," accessed on February 10, 2020, http://www.oais.info/.
22. "The Trustworthy Repositories Audit and Certification: Criteria and Checklist," accessed on February 10, 2020, https://www.crl.edu/sites/default/files/d6/attachments/pages/trac_0.pdf.
23. "Curation Lifecycle Model," *Digital Curation Conference*, accessed on February 10, 2020, https://www.dcc.ac.uk/guidance/curation-lifecycle-model.
24. Erin Baucom, Carol Kussmann, Amy Rudersdorf, Ozhan Saglik, Walker Sampson, and David Underdown, "Using Levels of Digital Preservation as an Assessment Tool," NDSA, 2019, accessed on February 10, 2020, https://osf.io/m6j4q/.
25. "Digital Preservation Capacity Maturity Model (DPCMM)," July 6, 2015, accessed on February 10, 2020, http://static1.squarespace.com/static/52ebbb45e4b06f07f8bb62bd/t/559bf956e4b06cac7e905011/1436285270565/DPCMM+Background+and+Performance+Metrics+v2.7_July+2015.pdf.
26. "CoreTrustSeal Trustworthy Data Repositories Requirements," *CoreTrustSeal*, accessed on February 10, 2020, https://www.coretrustseal.org/why-certification/requirements/.
27. "The Digital Preservation Coalition Rapid Assessment Model," *Digital Preservation Coalition*, September 2019, accessed on February 10, 2020, https://www.dpconline.org/docs/miscellaneous/our-work/dpc-ram/2006-dpc-ram-v-1-0/file.
28. "Digital Repository Audit Method Based in Risk Assessment," accessed on February 10, 2020, http://www.repositoryaudit.eu/.
29. Gillian Oliver and Ross Harvey, *Digital Curation* (Chicago: Neal-Schuman, 2016), 83–84.
30. Corrado and Sandy, *Digital Preservation for Libraries*, 119.
31. Smallwood, *Information Governance*, 46–48.
32. Franks, *Records and Information Management*, 123–25.
33. Smallwood, *Information Governance*, 102.

34. Kowalczyk, *Digital Curation for Libraries and Archives*, 25–26.
35. Oliver and Harvey, *Digital Curation*, 89–90.
36. Corrado and Sandy, *Digital Preservation for Libraries*, 124.
37. Ibid., 33.
38. Ricky Erway, *You've Got to Walk Before You Can Run: First Steps For Managing Born-Digital Content Received on Physical Media* (Dublin, OH: OCLC Research, 2012), 4.
39. Kowalczyk, *Digital Curation for Libraries and Archives*, 156.
40. Durant, "Preservation Assessments," 184–85.
41. Ibid.
42. Kowalczyk, *Digital Curation for Libraries and Archives*, 164; Kelly and Smith, "Assessing Collections Holistically," 50–53.
43. Dollar and Ashley, "Digital Preservation Capability Maturity Model," 4.

CHAPTER THREE

Digital Strategy

A Phased Approach to Building Capacity and Capabilities

Ideally, digital-stewardship assessment informs an enterprise digital strategy focused on the creation, management, and long-term accessibility of digital assets. As a cornerstone of planning and sustainable development, digital strategy connects the present, as defined by the digital-stewardship assessment, with the future roadmap. Every library, archive, and museum should have a digital strategy, regardless of its size or resource level, because digital collections across GLAM institutions are growing at an exponential rate and becoming more heterogenous, varied, dynamic, and distributed. Challenges abound for GLAM institutions that are often overwhelmed by the thought of managing the growing scope and size of digital assets in the context of shrinking budgets. Due to the diversity and size of digital collections, an institution needs a single vision for managing digital assets.

Many GLAM institutions lack digital leadership and, as a result, struggle to fully articulate a clear digital strategy because the digital ecosystem is dynamic and information technology is emergent and iterative, and change management is often influenced by evolving organizational capacities.[1] In many ways, a stewardship strategy is about digital leadership. In this context, a digital strategy is not contained to one initiative or a yearly goal or a grant-based project. Rather, a digital strategy is a continual process of adapting to changing environments and technological innovations. With the end goal of redefining the relevancy of GLAM sector services, a digital-stewardship strategy outlines a phased approach to continuous assessment, alignment, and realignment.[2]

Digital Leadership

Given the urgency of what seems like a herculean task, many librarians, archivists, and museum curators find themselves implementing digital stewardship by a piecemeal approach or in pockets within an organization, without having a firm grasp on how to sustain these initiatives given the exponential growth of digital assets. As staff grapple with the challenges of implementing good tenets of digital stewardship, many institutions experience a widening chasm between administrators and practitioners who become discouraged by the lack of a unified approach between "what is possible" and "what is doable." Most archivists, librarians, and curators realize that digital stewardship is not something an individual can do on their own, but rather something that requires support at all levels, with significant organizational realignment to address new hurdles relating to resource development and expanding digital competencies among staff members who are already working at capacity.

Given the widening gulf between practitioners and upper administration, GLAM sector leaders must be able to articulate a digital-stewardship vision that is guided by a strategic roadmap for purposeful and impactful uses of technology. In his analysis of changing paradigms in higher education, Eric Sheninger describes digital leadership as the ability to initiate sustainable change in order to ready institutions to adapt and embrace needed shifts to practice. Equally as important in the context of GLAM institutions, digital leadership is critical in cultivating and leveraging existing strengths and setting a course for adaptable shifts to digital-stewardship practices while anticipating future challenges. For digital leaders, a strategic mindset is essential in leveraging available resources to improve the current state while anticipating the changes that will empower institutions to commit to purposeful uses of technology. In many ways digital leadership is about advocating for the realignment of existing resources with emerging technologies in order to help institutions anticipate needs and establish direction in the context of an everchanging digital landscape.[3]

In this context, a critical component of a digital strategy is building capacity with a specific focus on budget and resource development. Resource-allocation strategies may include budget restructuring in the areas of capital investment, project funding, and the reallocation of operational funds. Capital investment, in the form of IT capital funds, ensure a stable infrastructure that is agile and evolves with the changing digital landscape. Although many GLAM institutions do not yet have capital campaigns focused on digital infrastructure development, more and more institutions will need to refine and redirect fundraising initiatives that connect institutional digital needs with the emerging tech sector as next-generation benefactors. Project funding, in the form of grants, can assist in tool and workflow development as well as training and building collection content. Grants and gifts should focus on filling in workflow gaps and developing professional competencies as opposed to major components of infrastructure, which may require significant resources for reinvestment, upgrades, and further development to ensure sustainability. Recurrent funding includes an increased allocation of operational capacity to maintain new digital services and ensure organizational realignment, as well as support new areas of digital stewardship activities. In addition to securing capital and project investments, recurrent funds may be drawn from existing and new operational resources that emerge from institutional reorganizations.[4]

For many GLAM institutions, a cohesive digital strategy involves a phased restructuring of collection programs and IT departments in order to align existing resources with the lifecycle management of digital collections. In this context, digital strategy is implemented through a series of phased stages that align and build-out existing resources over time and can be adapted and changed, allowing institutions to "pivot" to react to changing resource levels and technological advances. For most GLAM institutions, digital strategy often encompasses the reconceptualization of traditional organizational structures that have been in place since the mid-twentieth century and have focused on the management of analog or print-based collections. Deconstructing these collection management approaches begins with identifying and understanding the changes that are required to manage digital assets, as well as how these changes can be streamlined and consolidated as part of a strategic approach to a digital-stewardship service model. In addition, strategic digital development requires embracing outward facing approaches that include gathering information from external sources, analyzing varied approaches of allied professions, and monitoring institutional performance in order to assess and identify specific areas for future action.[5]

Infrastructure Development and Modular Design

Central to any digital strategy is the investment in system infrastructure, as it provides interoperable and scalable services with governance business models to support the management and preservation of digital assets at an enterprise level. Digital infrastructure will vary from institution to institution. However, for most GLAM institutions, digital ecosystems are based on a distributed service architecture. Specifically, DAME development supports discrete collection-management roles, which are handled by a network of interrelated applications, each one suited for the role it plays. In this context, the infrastructure needs to be robust enough to manage the scope and scale of a diverse digital-asset ecosystem but also flexible enough to accommodate the needs of various stakeholders. It also should include secure centralized storage, scalable networking, and an effective disaster-recovery plan.[6]

Modular design is a critical component to digital infrastructure for GLAM institutions. A digital strategy should include planning for system integration, which ensures the ease with which collection-management functions and workflows can be linked or coordinated with other systems along a spectrum of applications that is broad and diverse.[7] Content and system integration include enterprise services that provide a set of core capabilities that institutions can leverage across many applications. Core content management capabilities form the foundation for a new generation of digital-asset management applications that are built on a top layer content-management framework, rather than built from the ground up as standalone applications. Modularity of design and system integration facilitates sharing metadata, unified search and retrieval, ease of moving assets across secured networks, and ensuring granularity of access and permission controls.[8]

Enterprise infrastructures may include digital assets management (DAM) or media asset management (MAM) systems, which exclusively deal with rich media and centralized graphic assets. A content management system or a document management system may steward administrative records and institutional data but may also include image and multimedia files. Collection-management systems and digital-preservation systems comprise the core functionality of descriptive metadata management and comprehensive environments for ensuring the long-term access, health, and preservation of digital assets. Most open-source and commercial DAMs, collection-management systems, and digital-preservation systems are highly scalable and capable of integration and synchronization to support an approach to a microservices infrastructure for a complex and varied ecosystem.[9]

Central to infrastructure development is the ability of any system to exchange data with other systems, using different hardware and software platforms, and data structures and interfaces.[10] This interoperability maximizes efficiencies by enforcing data standards, normalizing inconsistencies, and consolidating data streams for ease in searchability.[11] Central to interoperability are application programming interfaces (APIs), which are protocols or a set of rules governing the format of data exchange between applications. For most web and cloud-based services, API management involves exposing business functions through application programming interfaces and integrating systems through cross-channel service virtualization using API gateways.[12] In addition, system management is reliant on the implementation of authentication protocols and access controls. With enterprise content management, authentication services can control access privileges, designate what users can see and what they can do with assets, as well as enable administrators to leverage access control or permission lists. In addition, two-way authentication protocols provide a single point of entry to mediate user access to a system, as well as mitigate the need for users to maintain separate logins for a number of applications.[13]

As GLAM institutions contemplate "building out" an interoperable infrastructure, DAME development should also provide a set of scalable general-purpose services accessible to varied organizational units, multiple repositories, and operating environments. Planning for a distributed, scalable solution architecture is critical for handling anticipated growth of digital assets over time.[14] In this context, scalability refers to the potential of a system to expand, as needed, based on the scope and scale of the ecosystem, which can range from an increased number of digital assets to the growth in the size of assets to the varied types or formats of assets.[15] Scalability is reliant on a distributed architecture that anticipates a high volume of assets, created and accessed by stakeholders, who are geographically distributed and work in different functional areas. Specifically, scale takes into consideration the number of units and end users that the system will serve, the volume of assets and transactions, and the diversity of data types and applications.[16]

To address the resources needed for building a scalable infrastructure, a digital strategy should include planning for the alignment between IT departments and collection-management staff, who work together to effect organizational change. In this context, digital strategy should encompass a set of actions that not only align digital-asset stewardship and IT resource management but also underscore the interrelatedness between collection-management processes and IT infrastructure, which ultimately strengthens the value of strategy-resource alignment necessary for sustainable approaches to institution-wide digital-asset management. In this context, digital strategy is implemented through a series of digital-stewardship processes that occur overtime and can be adapted, changed, scaled up, or scaled down.[17]

A major obstacle in realizing this vision has been the traditional positioning of IT departments or units in distinct clusters, either within or outside GLAM institutions. In this context, an IT department's primary role is implementing and maintaining information technology infrastructure, software, and storage architecture with less of a focus on strategic planning as it relates to digital content management. A digital strategy should explicitly recognize the embeddedness of IT throughout the organization and plan for their expanded role in identifying opportunities for the implementation of emerging technologies as part of a digital-stewardship service model.[18] In other words, a digital strategy should facilitate multifunctional, simultaneous development and reconfiguration of IT resources across multiple digital-stewardship management processes.[19]

When building a framework for enterprise digital-asset management, the blurring distinction between collection management and IT departments often leads to the fusion between the areas.[20] At a very high level, a digital strategy should solidify principles that apply to all digital collections. A digital strategy often begins with infrastructure development, technology funding, and a long-term institutional commitment to the principles of good digital stewardship, but much of the work of implementing the strategy focuses on calibrating actions to mobilize IT resources to leverage technology across multiple organizational components in the area of collection management.[21] Elements of the convergence of IT and collection management include leveraging a minimal level of description for digital assets; prioritizing the scope and scale of the digitization of analog content; careful consideration of the acquisition of born-digital content; a commitment to accessibility, discovery, usability, and reusability of digital assets; shared responsibility of digital-rights management; as well as embracing innovative approaches to digital-collections sustainability.[22]

Advancing New Organizational Program Models

In addition to a greater investment in digital infrastructure, new collaborative organizational structures are emerging as libraries, museums, and archives confront the challenge of building digital capacities and capabilities with existing resources. Organizational challenges include a lack of expertise and knowledge gaps, organizational inertia, and technology dependency, as well as addressing cultural change that requires staff to navigate the continuity of existing processes with new workflows, resources, and technology. Reframing an institutional mission around a holistic digital-stewardship model often requires a reconceptualization of organizational structures and program models that intentionally reconfigure the resource base while putting existing resources to new uses.[23] As libraries, archives, and museums contemplate an enterprise digital strategy for a growing number of digitized surrogates, born-digital assets, and research data, institutions understand that these expanding needs can only be met by more flexible approaches to work, as well as organizational agility undertaken through job redesign, training, and reorganization. These new organizational structures also accompany new leadership frameworks in response to changing service models, advances in information technology, and the need for active and systematic collaborations both within and outside the organization. For most GLAM institutions, this new framework for digital leadership should empower administrators to articulate an accessible, comprehensive strategy that can be shared broadly, complete with a vision that advocates for digital empowerment throughout the organization.[24]

For GLAM leadership, a digital strategy begins with aligning digital stewardship as a core service that encompasses functional responsibilities that extend more comprehensively to collection management of a full range of cultural heritage and research assets. While a great number of librarians, archivists, and curators understand that GLAM institutions are managing more digital collections, there are still a number of GLAM staff members who believe that digital stewardship is "in addition to" the core services of selecting, acquiring, and cataloging analog collections.[25] In this context, librarians, archivists, and curators need to evolve their collection-management practices, which are grounded in managing traditional analog content, and, instead, develop new capabilities to manage new forms of scholarship, cultural artifacts, distinctive primary source material, and research data.[26]

A critical first step to this vision begins with embracing organizational structures that promote more intentional function-based digital services that minimize collection and service silos. To successfully achieve this new collection-management service model, many libraries, museums and archives are aligning subject curatorial and distinctive collections staff and services more holistically into larger digital initiatives and organizational structures. These new organizational models are framed by programmatic structures that support blended positions, cross-functional workflows, distinctive collections teams, and digital project management, as well as integrated digital collections management. These organizational refinements, in the area of distinctive collections, are changing the collection landscape for GLAM institutions with the goal of accommodating access and discovery at scale, ushering in new service models for print and analog-based collections, and supporting the "surfacing" or mainstreaming of local, unique, and distinctive collections for broader audiences.[27]

From Subject Curators to Functional Specialists

Central to these organizational changes within GLAM institutions is a gradual shift from subject curatorial–based roles to more functional-based positions with a focus on mainstreaming distinctive collections. As information technology reshapes the approach to digital stewardship as well as collection use, there is a greater urgency to deconstruct traditional parameters that have distinguished distinctive and unique collections and services into siloed collection spaces. With these changes, archivists, librarians, and museum curators have had to reexamine longstanding assumptions relating to collection care, which has been grounded in traditional education and professional training, long-held organizational structures, and mid-century approaches to collection-management and research services, as well as in the contours of GLAM professional history and work culture.

Historically, distinctive collections have tended to be highly independent organizational units because the nature of specialized materials require a close mediation that is guided by subject expertise within a curatorial-based organizational structure that situates and fortifies institutional knowledge of collections within a unit and, more specifically, with one person. Additionally, subject-based curatorial responsibilities often focus on the physicality of collection care and analog preservation. For many special collections, museums, and archives, subject-based positions focus on highlighting the special expertise required in not only servicing collections in physical reading rooms but also for the collection management of unique primary sources, which are housed and managed in environmentally controlled, secure collection spaces. In this context, a curator's focus is inward—the physical stewardship of collections as well as honing a subject specialization based on highly mediated encounters in physical spaces. Increasingly, the need for subject specializations within libraries, museums, and archives is being met by distinctive collection teams with a technical functional-base expertise framed by principles of digital stewardship.[28]

In recent years, academic libraries, in particular, have seen similar parallel transformations with subject selectors' roles. As a result, libraries are moving away from a collection development liaison model in favor of more functional-related positions focusing on research and engagement, metadata management, and the widening umbrella of "digital initiatives." This shift reflects the academic liaison's ever-broadening range of duties, including proficiencies with emerging digital literacies, course-embedded research support, individual research consultations, data management, and digital humanities specializations. This shift also requires greater flexibility to allow the institution to "pivot" with the evolving needs of the institution's users. The rise of functional-based positions represents the need for a more sustainable approach to organizational development that enables agility in personnel resources and a broader view of collection management that incorporates digital strategies and stewardship activities early in the lifecycle management of digital assets. This functional-based model also requires new skill development at unit and program levels, as collection librarians, museum curators, and archivists move away from position descriptions focused solely on subject expertise and toward specialized areas that highlight functional knowledge and technical and digital expertise.[29]

In addition, an emphasis on blended positions is an important means in building an institutional culture that emphasizes versatility, collaborations, and collective problem-solving in the area of digital collections management. Blended positions require librarians, museum curators, and archivists to tap into their abilities to see connections and relate across areas of expertise to more effectively engage functionally throughout the institution. By fostering an integrative approach to digital work that extends beyond departmental borders, special collections librarians, archivists, and museum curators can share outward-facing strategies for "inviting in" functional specialists to work with and expand the reach of distinctive collections beyond the physical confines of in-house reading rooms and exhibit spaces.

Distinctive Collection Teams: A New Leadership Framework

In addition to crafting new, functional-based positions, integrating existing faculty and staff into cross-functional teams also reinforces a collaborative model for digital stewardship across libraries, archives, and museums. More specifically, the growing emphasis on digital-project management has been the impetus for a new leadership framework for the GLAM sector that empowers "distinctive collection teams" to facilitate collaborative problem-solving. For those who do not have the resources for dedicated digital-project managers, integrated team building fosters opportunities for librarians, curators, and archivists to work on content selection with acquisition librarians and museum curators, as well as to expand their sense of existing collection strengths more holistically as they work with faculty and staff who specialize in scholarly communication, metadata creation, data curation, digitization services, and digital scholarship. In addition to encouraging more collaborative organizational structures, opportunities to strengthen digital-project management offer libraries, archives, and museums important opportunities to foster professional development of staff, especially as it relates to building out digital-stewardship capacity and capabilities.[30]

Distinctive collection teams can also work on digital-collection development policies to guide acquisition of digital content, which is an essential component of good digital stewardship. A collection policy defines the scope of collecting responsibilities, assists in integrating digital curation in early lifecycle management of digital assets, and defines the set of digital assets for which GLAM institutions will assume long-term curatorial responsibility. In addition to defining appropriate levels of responsibilities for preservation and access, digital-collection development policies should also outline digital content of only temporary value as well as digital assets hosted for access purposes only. Closely associated with defining the scope of digital collections, policies should address roles, responsibilities, and workflows, as well as the contours of asset deposit, submission agreements, donor contracts and gift agreements, and purchased acquisitions. A separate section should be devoted to licensed resources focusing on access and preservation responsibilities that may range from perpetual access clauses to shared custody agreements that address lifecycle costs and stipulate who is responsible for preserving assets after the dissolution of licensing contracts. A digital-collection development policy should cover agreements with commercial service providers specifically outlining digital-preservation specifications and storage and access requirements. In addition, the policy may need to reference cooperative agreements for distributed collecting and include submission guidelines for research data-management purposes. Finally, digital-collection development policies should address the contours for web archiving, specifically clarifying the scope of collecting initiatives as well as the rights to collect copies of U.S.-based and international websites under the copyright deposit law.[31]

Professional Development as Organizational Realignment

Leveraging professional development is essential in expanding digital expertise across the organization and a critical component of a digital strategy. For the GLAM sector, the challenge of responding to organizational change is that the roles and responsibilities of librarians, curators, and archivists are constantly evolving. As such, the faculty and staff of GLAM institutions have to be "change ready"—open, adaptable, and flexible. For many institutions, expertise with the lifecycle management of digital assets represent new skills for most librarians, archivists, and curators. In order to expand these skill sets, professional development is critical to support new technical competencies and workforce agility in managing digital assets at an enterprise level.

With a focus on expanding digital competencies, digital leadership should advocate for professional development opportunities as an important strategic investment that fosters the necessary skills related to the work of digital stewardship, including the management of digital-preservation environments, as well as the design and development of information systems, infrastructure, and storage architecture.[32] Professional development may range from reviewing and rewriting existing job descriptions to providing continuing professional development funds to accommodating changing roles that encourage more creative and innovative outlets for professional growth. Onsite workshops, certification programs, webinars, learning modules, continuing education programs, and personalized learning pathways offer opportunities to raise technical competencies.[33]

As the digital environment becomes more complex, functional-based skills in the areas of digital curation will be essential as GLAM staff engage in managing a diverse range of digital assets. In order to ensure breadth and depth in digital expertise, GLAM institutions may want to provide multiple levels of professional development that range from fostering a common foundational understanding of digital stewardship to focusing on advancing skills needed to support system-thinking and organization gaps identified as part of a digital-stewardship assessment. At a basic level, professional development opportunities should have a cross-functional approach to address the broad collective challenges faced by entire staffs of GLAM institutions. This will enable a culture of digital advocacy with a common vocabulary. At a more in-depth level, opportunities for digital practitioners should encompass roles that support patterns of thinking and working with data, information, artifacts, and infrastructures that exist in a shifting landscape of ever-changing job profiles and career paths. Building practical skills through certificate programs and continuing education is essential to develop competencies that help institutions build digital capacity. Opportunities aimed at digital stewards, or those practitioners who will be engaging in digital curation and preservation work, should encompass the greatest percentage of professional organizational funds and focus on advanced skills as needed for the performance of a wide range of digital-stewardship duties necessary to support integrative workflows.

The long-term success of digital stewardship depends not only on fostering new talent but also on recruiting emerging professionals from outside and within an institution for new leadership positions. Nurturing next-generation digital leadership is a critical component of a digital strategy

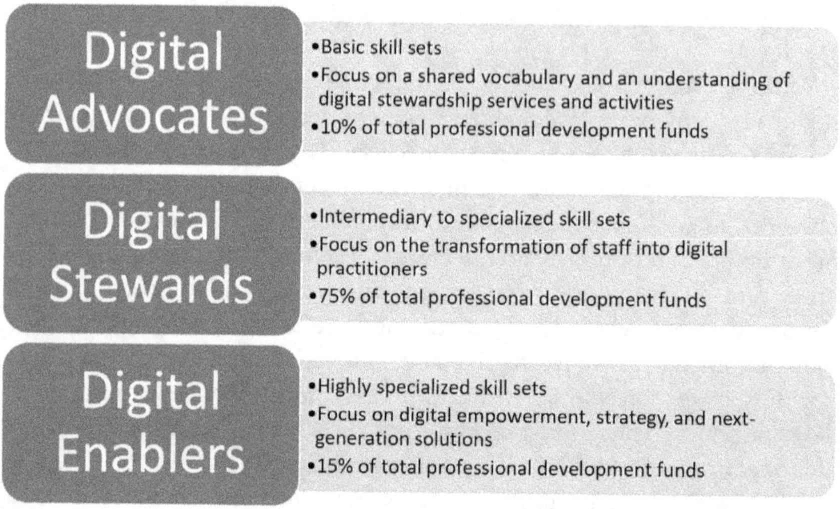

Digital Advocates
- Basic skill sets
- Focus on a shared vocabulary and an understanding of digital stewardship services and activities
- 10% of total professional development funds

Digital Stewards
- Intermediary to specialized skill sets
- Focus on the transformation of staff into digital practitioners
- 75% of total professional development funds

Digital Enablers
- Highly specialized skill sets
- Focus on digital empowerment, strategy, and next-generation solutions
- 15% of total professional development funds

Figure 3.1. Levels of Professional Development to Enhance Digital-Stewardship Capacity

and essential to organizational innovation. These leaders serve as "digital enablers" whose roles encompass assessing, deploying, and training others in existing technologies, as well as recommending emerging technologies to expand DAME development. Digital enablers address perhaps the biggest challenge for the GLAM sector by repositioning staffs to think beyond core services to preserving a diverse ecosystem of data, made meaningful in a variety of contexts and accessible through unified discovery platforms for use in virtual learning and public engagement environments. At the most advanced level of professional development, digital enablers, who work on designing the digital assessment management ecosystem, should have opportunities to build their operational knowledge of organizational culture as well as an understanding of how to connect with communities of data creators and users in order to serve the critical need of establishing organizational building blocks for sustainable digital stewardship.[34]

It is important to note that a digital strategy is not a top-down mandate nor does it lend itself to "a one-size-fits-all solution." It is not about reorganization as much as it is about realignment of information technology, collections management, and professional development with the distinct needs of an institution's collections and the scope and scale of available resources. Digital-stewardship approaches should be determined by open discussions around shared policies, shared values and practices, a culture of continuous improvement, and foresight planning based on collection growth and collaborative funding approaches. As most libraries, archives, and museums face slimmed-down budgets and fewer personnel as a result of early retirements, a digital strategy is a framework to reconceptualize, regroup, and rearticulate the most efficient ways to accomplish a holistic approach to digital stewardship with a focus on intentional decisions that serve to foster leadership development, strategic innovation, reallocation of resources, and staff support.

Notes

1. Adrian Yeow, Christina Soh, and Rina Hansen, "Aligning with a New Digital Strategy: A Dynamic Capabilities Approach," *Journal of Strategic Information Systems* 27 (2018): 44–45.

2. Ibid.

3. Eric Sheninger, *Digital Leadership: Changing Paradigms for Changing Times* (Thousand Oaks, CA: Corwin, 2019), xvi, xviii, xix, xxiii.

4. "University of Oxford Gardens, Libraries, Museums Digital Strategy," accessed on September 10, 2020, https://www.glam.ox.ac.uk/sites/default/files/glam/documents/media/GLAM%20Digital%20Strategy%202016.pdf.

5. Ibid.; Yeow et al., "Aligning with a New Digital Strategy," 44–45.

6. Stacy Kowalczyk, *Digital Curation for Libraries and Archives* (Santa Barbara, CA: Libraries Unlimited, 2018), 121–22.

7. Mark Walter, "Architectural Considerations in Digital Asset Management," *The Gilbane Report*, October 5, 2004, 4–5, accessed on September 10, 2020, https://gilbane.com/wp-content/uploads/2020/01/GilbaneWP_StellentIBM_1.0.pdf.

8. Ibid., 2.

9. Shailesh Kumar Shivakumar, *Enterprise Content and Search Management for Building Digital Platforms* (Hoboken, NJ: Wiley, 2016), 15–16, 24–26, 111.

10. Kowalczyk, *Digital Curation for Libraries and Archives*, 111.

11. Ibid., 128.

12. Walter, "Architectural Considerations in Digital Asset Management," 4.

13. Ibid.

14. Shivakumar, *Enterprise Content and Search Management*, 15.

15. Kowalczyk, *Digital Curation for Libraries and Archives*, 111.

16. Walter, "Architectural Considerations in Digital Asset Management," 16.

17. Yeow et al., "Aligning with a New Digital Strategy," 44.

18. Dale Askey and Lisa Janicke Hinchliffe. "Finding a Way from the Margins to the Middle: Library Information Technology, Leadership and Culture," *Ithaka-SR Issue Brief*, May 18, 2017, accessed on September 10, 2020, https://sr.ithaka.org/publications/finding-a-way-from-the-margins-to-the-middle/.

19. Yeow et al., "Aligning with a New Digital Strategy," 44–45.

20. Ibid.

21. Ibid., 46.

22. Katharine Schopflin, "Information Management Approaches to Digital Asset Management: A Case Study in Success and Failure," *Journal of Digital Media Management* 3–4 (2015): 311.

23. Yeow et al., "Aligning with a New Digital Strategy," 46.

24. Deanna B. Marcum, "Library Leadership for the Digital Age," *Information Services and Uses* 36 (2016): 106.

25. Ibid., 108.

26. Olga Y. Rieger, "What's a Collection Anyway?" *Ithaka-SR Issue Brief*, June 6, 2019, accessed on September 10, 2020, https://sr.ithaka.org/publications/whats-a-collection-anyway/.

27. Ibid.

28. Angela Fritz, "From Collection Silos to Digital Content Hubs: Digital Project Management in Special Collections and University Archives," in *Project Management in the Library Workplace (Advances in Library Administration and Organization, vol. 38)*, eds. Alice Daugherty and Samantha Schmehl Hines (Bingley, United Kingdom: Emerald Publishing, 2018): 192–93.

29. Danielle Cooper and Roger C. Schonfeld, "Rethinking Liaison Programs for the Humanities," *Ithaka-SR Issue Brief*, July 26, 2017, accessed on September 10, 2020, https://sr.ithaka.org/publications/rethinking-liaison-programs-for-the-humanities/; Janice M. Jaguszewski and Karen Williams, "New Roles for New Times: Transforming Liaison Roles in Academic Libraries," *Association of Research Libraries*, August 2013, accessed on September 10, 2020, https://www.arl.org/wp-content/uploads/2015/12/nrnt-liaison-roles-revised.pdf.

30. Fritz, "From Collection Silos to Digital Content Hubs," 192–93.

31. Library of Congress, *LC21: A Digital Strategy for the Library of Congress* (Washington DC: National Academy Press, 2000), 5–8.

32. Hannah Lewi, Wally Smith, Dirk vom Lehn, and Steven Cooke, *The Routledge International Handbook of New Digital Practices in Galleries, Libraries, Archives, Museums, and Heritage Sites* (New York: Routledge, 2019), 1.

33. For articles on GLAM professional development programs, see Bruce Fulton, Peter Botticelli, and Jana Bradley, "Digin: A Hands-On Approach to a Digital Curation Curriculum for Professional Development," *Journal of Education for Library and Information Science* 52, no. 2 (April 1, 2011): 95–109; Jaya Raju, "Informational Professionals or IT Professional?: The Knowledge and Skills Required by Academic Librarians in the Digital Library Environment," *Portal* 14, no. 4 (October 2017): 739; "Building Professional Development Opportunities in Data Sciences for Academic Librarians," *IFLA Journal* 43, no. 1 (March 2017): 65–80; "The Role of Administrators in Professional Development: Considerations for Facilitating Learning Among Academic Librarians," *Journal of Library Administration* 58, no. 5 (July 4, 2018): 407–33; Jez Cope and James Baker, "Library Carpentry: Software Skills Training for Library Professionals," *Journal of Digital Curation* 12, no. 2 (May 1, 2018); Joyce Ray, "Digital Curation in Museums," *Hi Tech* 35, no. 1 (March 20, 2017): 32–39;

Yuanyuan Feng and Lorraine Richards, "A Review of Digital Curation Professional Competencies: Theory and Current Practices," *Records Management Journal* 28, no. 1 (March 19, 2018): 62–78.

34. Sue McKnight, "Here Today and Here Tomorrow," in *University Libraries and Digital Learning Environments*, eds. Penny Dale, Jill Beard, and Matt Holland (New York: Routledge, 2016), 10.

CHAPTER FOUR

Integrative Collections Management
Streamlining Digital Stewardship

For GLAM institutions, a digital strategy outlines the roadmap for integrative collection-management policies and cross-functional curatorial activities. Framed by a digital-stewardship assessment, an enterprise strategy should foster collaborative approaches to content creation and collections management that facilitate cost-effective and sustainable workflows. In many ways, these changing approaches to collections management serve as defining moments for the GLAM sector to accelerate their own transformation through collaborative action and innovative services. The challenge for many institutions in realizing this service model is that GLAM organizational structures and collections-management approaches have not always been able to adjust to changing expectations around the accessibility and universal discovery of digital assets at an enterprise level. The key to libraries', museums', and archives' future work will be how quickly they can reorientate workflows to accommodate a much more refined definition of "digital-collections management" in order to facilitate pathways to multiply delivery platforms that will meet the evolving needs of broad user communities.[1]

Convergence of IT and Collections Management in DAME Development

One of the main challenges that has led libraries, museums, and archives to turn toward more integrated collections management is a result of society's ability to generate data. With the exponential growth of digital assets, data production has outpaced the ability of libraries, archives, and museums to make optimal use of these assets for knowledge discovery, research, and public engagement. In addition to the sheer volume, and often redundant nature of born-digital materials, ownership and responsibility to care for digital assets is often vague due to a lack of digital-rights management. Other challenges include the heterogeneity of assets, particularly of legacy formats, the increased complexity relating to documenting the provenance and context of these assets through associated descriptive metadata, as well as the proliferation of dynamic files with multiple components, which may make it difficult to accurately render the content in aggregate over time. More often, archivists, museum curators, and librarians are confronted by increasing scale of large files that stress the existing technological infrastructure due to requirements for faster processing speeds and higher bandwidth network connections to move files. In addition, GLAM institutions are contemplating the budgetary challanges of increased storage needs to manage the replication of multiple files as part of digital-preservation workflows.[2]

To address these challenges, the conceptual model of holistic digital stewardship fosters the convergence of collections-management units and IT departments whose close collaborations reinforce the connection between system design and the use and reuse of research data, digital collections, and cultural heritage assets. Guided by tenets of digital stewardship, IT departments and GLAM units share the responsibilities of managing hardware and software, evaluating and implementing digital-collections management through "software as a service" solutions and cloud computing, and sharing the benefits of applications that are hosted by proprietary services, which allow IT professionals time to devote to DAME development initiatives that are unique to the needs of the institution. In this context, the convergence of IT and GLAM stewardship units facilitates the entire spectrum of digital-stewardship activities and merges museum, archives, and library collection-management functions relating to acquisitions, processing, cataloging, and preservation services. Due to the diverse range of assets, these partnerships also support metadata and rights management, as well as the development of cross-functional workflows in order to maximize efficiencies at an enterprise level.[3] As outlined in chapter 1, the concept of a DAME evolved as a result of the need for integrative solutions to streamline the access and preservation of a myriad of digital assets created, managed, and maintained by siloed units, departments, and programs within the same institution. Integrated collections management is central to the development of the DAME as it consolidates these digital assets from various enterprise sources into a unified information architecture.[4]

In this context, collaborations between IT and collections-management units promote more unified approaches to DAME development, where digital-stewardship activities occur early in the lifecycle management of digital assets. In addition, a DAME often promotes unmediated or self-service deposit models, facilitates unified discovery, and secures content through defined authentication protocols and authorized permission roles, as well as ensures the management of content in a normalized, structured format so that assets are accessible across various applications and services. Finally, a DAME leverages technology to enable collections-management teams to collaborate, create, manage, curate, deliver, and archive digital assets. And it drives changes to organizational models and programmatic work structures that facilitate cross-functional workflows with the purpose of distributing and storing digital assets in a centrally managed infrastructure.[5]

It is important to note that a DAME is not one tool or one discrete system but rather multiple tools, software components, and storage architecture and services that are combined to perform active management and end-to-end digital-stewardship processes.[6] In order to accommodate the convergence of data, the DAME allows institutions to cease to think about their collections as discrete digital objects and, instead, requires the management of digital assets in a defined ecosystem. This reconceptualization is important because it implies a larger investment in digital stewardship with the recognition that long-term value of assets resides in the ability to promote universal discovery and reuse of digital collections for broader user communities.[7]

A Unified Approach to Digital Preservation and Early Intervention

Central to integrated collections management is a unified approach to digital preservation that enables responsible digital stewardship across the organization while aligning tool selection and infrastructure development with the overall digital strategy. Rather than focusing on collections-management rules and curatorial oversight and decision-making, a sound digital-preservation policy provides a structure for "organizational thinking" on ways to embed digital stewardship and integrated collections management across the institution.[8] Successful digital preservation cannot be accomplished by a single individual or even a single department. It requires a series of managed activities encompassing more integrated technical and curatorial workflows. Requiring a high level of cooperation across departments and functional roles, unified digital-preservation services are reliant on standardized workflows that facilitate the "packaging" of metadata with the digital object as well as automated storage pathways that enable geographically diverse distribution of digital assets in closely monitored digital-preservation storage environments.

Strategies for unified digital preservation include providing appraisal guidance for asset creators, gaining physical and intellectual control over current holdings, and conducting ongoing risk assessment, specifically as it relates to preservation format sustainability. Additionally, a scalable, flexible architecture, a greater focus on automation in the processing of digital collections, and the adoption of microservices associated with digital-preservation systems are important foundational components for more unified approaches to digital preservation.[9] By transforming files into sustainable preservation formats and maintaining usable access derivatives, unified digital-preservation workflows protect the authenticity, integrity, and usability of digital assets. At the same time, these workflows standardize digital-stewardship practices by documenting collections-management decision points and encouraging transparency and shared authority for the centralized management of digital assets across the institution.[10]

Integrated Collections Management Defined

In the context of integrated collections management, a variety of units share the work of stewarding digital collections. Ideally, these teams are operationally integrated throughout the organization, working together to pursue common goals and outcomes to ensure broad accessibility of digital assets while establishing sustainable digital-stewardship environments that situate long-term management of digital collections at an enterprise level. In order to meet the challenges of streamlining and surfacing distinctive digital collections, multimedia assets, and research data, integrated collections management requires the adoption of an enterprise digital strategy that serves to refine cross-functional workflows within new organizational structures, as well as creates overarching policies and conceptual models around a range of tools, software, and information systems that support the institution's larger DAME.[11] In addition, integrated collections management facilitates the consolidation of technical services and IT silos in order to reduce redundancies and streamline acquisitions, processing, and cataloging activities with other units in the organization.[12]

As the information landscape changes, librarians, archivists, and museum curators are central to the implementation of new digital practices with more integrative collections-management approaches in mind. For example, as in-house digital initiatives have grown in size and scope, librarians in technical services have assessed the workflows and traditional staffing models that were previously dedicated to maintaining print collections, specifically monograph cataloging, and instead have focused on the integration of archival and distinctive collections, research datasets, e-resources, rich media, and born-digital materials into libraries' collections-management policies and workflows. Additional examples of integrative collections management include:

- the realignment of museum registration and archival accessioning and processing with library acquisitions and cataloging
- the creation of cross-functional collections-management and technical service workflows that include expansive metadata services and remediation projects
- the repositioning of monograph catalogers in the areas of finding aid production, archival processing, and pre-ingest/ingest workflows for digital collections
- the creation of cross-functional digitization workflows with "value-added" distributed metadata services that encompass the staff of special collections, university archives, technical services, museum registration, and collection development
- the downsizing of analog archival processing units for born-digital processing workstations located throughout collections-management areas
- the integration of expediated technical appraisal methodologies as part of pre-ingest workflows for a range of digital content
- a greater focus on the integration of "digitization on demand" for all print and analog collections with "curation-ready" digital-preservation workflows and unified discovery paths
- the integration of collection development with teaching and learning units
- the integration of reference and research public service points for distinctive collections through a central, virtual reading room
- the consolidation of collection space for distinctive collections in order to position GLAM institutions for cooperative collecting and collaborative collection efforts on a national and international level

Although these areas of consolidation may differ from institution to institution, integrative collections management is an essential component of a sustainable digital strategy because it brings together the work of librarians, curators, and archivists across divisions and institutions into more central points of engagement for the collection care and unified preservation of unique digital assets.

Cross-Functional Workflows and "Curation-Ready" Assets

In the context of a digital-stewardship framework, workflow development is critical to ensure early intervention in the lifecycle management of digital assets. Workflow development also enables standard approaches to the submission, ingest, and management of digital assets, which is essential for cost-effective approaches to preserving and facilitating discovery to diverse digital content.[13] Most importantly, effective workflows connect the work of GLAM staff to DAME development in order to enhance the quality of metadata, reduce costs for capture and ingest, and mitigate redundancies in stewardship processes and storage locations. Cross-functional workflows serve to unify several different information systems as well as units, programs, and individuals who may have worked separately from each other.[14] In addition, the design of a modular-based DAME facilitates the transition of siloed data-management approaches to a more open, networked infrastructure that may facilitate the automation of workflows when appropriate. The design and implementation of integrated, cross-functional workflows should be:

- *responsive to collection needs.* Workflow development should balance the needs of unique collections with standardized work processes. Ideally, collections-management workflows should articulate the long-term value of assets, avoid duplication of services, ensure accountability of stewardship activities, and encourage a shared understanding and consensus around collection care and management.[15]
- *role-based.* A term often used by IT professionals, a "role" refers to a class of users who perform a specific type of work task. Most often, roles designate work tasks to specific units and outline how units and people fit into workflows. It is important to note that roles within workflows should remain stable even as individuals' positions may change.
- *flexible.* Workflows should not only accommodate the unique needs of a range of digital assets within an ecosystem but should also be adaptable to changing contexts and resource levels. At the same time, workflows should also be flexible and scalable, allowing GLAM staff to embrace new technologies and tools as they become available.
- *transparent.* Workflows should be well-documented and in-action, allowing all users to know when an asset moves from one stage to the next. Workflows should specify where information goes, what form it takes, and who performs each task.

- *commensurate with resources.* Workflows should match available resources and allow for appropriate scoping and scaling as an institution "builds out" capacity.
- *efficient.* Workflows should be based on an analysis of both the business processes that an institution wants to streamline and the current resources available to accomplish the work. Good workflows should help facilitate digital-stewardship activities. If workflows increase project queues and hinder work from being accomplished, it most likely means that the workflows are not aligned with available resources.
- *standards-based.* Workflows should reflect formal and informal best practices agreed upon by professional organizations or local communities of practice. Standards are essential in maintaining a level of common practice that ensures quality or consistency of work-based processes.
- *secure.* Workflows should be framed by two-way authentication and permission management in order to ensure data integrity as well as compliance with information security standards relating to access, handling, transfer, and storage of digital assets.
- *measurable.* Workflows should generate measures to analyze their effectiveness.[16]

These workflow principles assist in leveraging information systems and tools to enable accuracy, semantic persistence, responsible stewardship, and

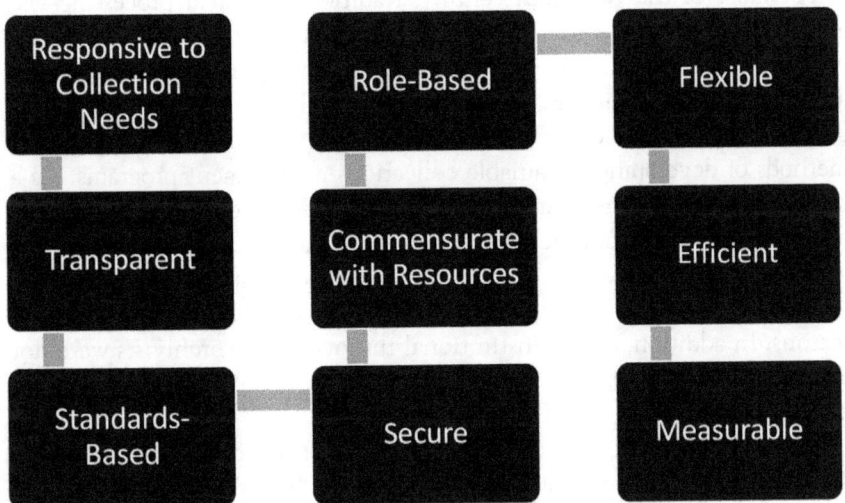

Figure 4.1. Considerations for Designing Cross-functional Workflows

accountability in managing digital assets at an enterprise level. Collections-management workflows, with designated roles and responsibilities, ensure data integrity with due attention to information governance, as well as security and access protocols. Finally, workflow development recognizes collection needs and associated processes that ensure certain crucial categories of assets are managed consistently across the organization. Carefully designed, cross-functional workflows and collaborative stewardship services, which may include integrated, shared, cloud-based work spaces, are essential in ensuring complete, meaningful, and useful assets over time.[17]

From Analog Archival Processing to Strategic Mass Digitization

In order to create cross-functional workflows, archivists, librarians, and curators have had to be more strategic in reevaluating traditional methods and approaches to collection care and management. Nowhere is this more important than in the area of analog archival processing. Historically, arrangement and description encompasses all the activities related to stewardship of analog archival content including maintaining context, ensuring appropriate care and continued access over time, as well as creating descriptive metadata in the form of finding aids and machine-readable catalog (MARC) records. Arrangement and description has long been the primary method of facilitating access to special collections and archives, and the professional methodologies that guide this work are grounded in history and historic precedent dating back to the French Revolution.

For most of the twentieth century, traditional archival processing was guided by the same three basic principles: provenance, collection-level control, and original order. Although these archival principles had provided archivists with a consistent, thorough, and thoughtful approach to servicing collections, these principles did not always give libraries and archives clear methods of developing sustainable collections-management programs. As a result, by the end of the twentieth century, most distinctive collections faced massive backlogs of unprocessed materials. While researchers could easily access processed collections, they often had no idea that unprocessed collections existed or were barred from using unprocessed collections for security reasons. In addition, due to institutional turnover, some archivists were not aware of the nature or historical significance of collections that languished in their backlog.

At the beginning of the twenty-first century it was clear that a new way of thinking about archival processing was needed. In 2004, Mark Greene and Dennis Meissner offered a radical solution in their article "More Product,

Less Process: Revamping Traditional Processing." This article was influential and thought-provoking because it caused archivists to recalibrate practices to meet twenty-first century processing challenges by offering new approaches and suggestions for more proactive arrangement and description practices to meet the varying needs of diverse analog collections. In addition to calling for more flexible concepts and approaches, the authors argued that processing goals should be "user-centered." They also outlined the challenges, given limited resources, of traditional detailed arrangement and description and argued that processing archivists have been largely hindered by impractical and rigid standards established and maintained by their own profession. Greene and Meissner's method, often referred to as "MPLP," after the article title, or "minimal processing," advocated that archives simplify processing collections at what they referred to as the "golden minimum." Since the publication of this article, archives and special collections have been strategically employing MPLP in their archival and special collections programs. And by way, these guidelines have empowered archivists to evaluate specific needs of each analog collection and make a series of sound professional decisions to promote a level of processing appropriate to each collection.

MPLP gave way to extensible processing, which included the use and reuse of descriptive metadata gathered during the assessment of unprocessed collections, the repurposing of accession data to create baseline collection descriptions for online discovery, and the large-scale or on-demand digitization of archival content as part of an archival processing plan. Outcomes and metrics that have been derived as part of extensible processing have allowed archivists the ability to integrate digitization assessment early in the lifecycle management of distinctive collections. For processing managers, MPLP and extensible processing have been important tools in developing more strategic approaches to setting priorities, restructuring workflows, and developing more robust accessioning programs, as well as significantly reducing analog archival processing backlogs.[18]

With the greater emphasis on integrated collections management, archives, libraries, and museums have continued to consolidate distinctive collection silos in order to reduce redundancies and streamline acquisitions, description, and processing activities with other units across the institution. In this context, key elements of integrative collections management include the reduction of staffing in large analog processing units and the realignment of archival accessioning and appraisal methodologies with library acquisition and metadata services in order to create cross-functional workflows with valued-added distributed metadata and unified digital preservation services for both digitized and born-digital content.

Selecting a Digitization Path

In the context of integrated collections management, digitization paths may encompass in-house digitization, outsourced digitization, or a combination of both. Selecting a digitization path is a critical component of digital collections management that can have significant implications for digital-stewardship service models and resource levels. As a growing component of GLAM ecosystems, digitization projects can encompass a wide array of analog formats and, as such, can be the impetus for building expertise, digital-stewardship workflows, and DAME infrastructure over time. Most GLAM institutions will have varied capacity for in-house digitization projects while strategically outsourcing digitization when appropriate. Before considering the digitization path, institutions should carefully weigh how the digital content may affect the ecosystem, specifically as it relates to available curatorial resources and digital-stewardship services. Although each project is unique, the decision to undertake digitization in-house or via a third party will depend on a variety of factors including but not limited to:

Table 4.1. Considerations for Digitization Paths

Factor	Definition	In-house Considerations	Outsource Considerations
Value	Uniqueness, intrinsic significance, or historical relevance	Secure, institution controls access, physical space, and environmental conditions	Verify security, transport methods, access protocols, and environmental controls
Condition	Fragile nature, "at-risk" formats	Curatorial expertise and oversight, specialized handling, and workflows based on the needs of the collection or items	Verify staff expertise and experience, as well as handling and preparation procedures, workflows, and equipment specifications
Size	Large, medium, or small collections or item-level counts	Small textual and photograph collections or digitization-on-demand based on reference or teaching requests	Large, print-based collections, sizable graphic and AV collections, or series within collections based on intrinsic or historic value

Factor	Definition	In-house Considerations	Outsource Considerations
Complexity	Format type, heavily annotated, multiple formats, interrelatedness to other digital content, and materials reliant on content or context curation	Unless in-house specialization, textual collections to build out digitization workflows; materials that require context-driven interpretations	Best for specialized or rare film, audio, and AV formats; oversized materials; and items that need little curatorial context
Cost	Cost of digitization per item, plus additional resources, personnel, equipment, and preservation storage	Best for small collections to build out workflows and resources and "on-demand" digitization research services	Budgeted cost per item with tiered pricing for specific formats, number of copies, extent of metadata services, as well as enhanced file processing and transcription
Timeframe	Time period to complete the digitization project	Long-term or ongoing print-based projects	Short-term projects, grant- or endowment-funded, projects that coincide with a milestone
Rights	Includes permissions relating to access and use	Reproduction rights for unpublished material unclear or unknown with reference to a take-down policy	Institution owns the rights, institution has permission from the rights holder, or items are in the public domain
Expertise	Level of specialization and skill sets required to complete high-quality digitization work	In-house specialization to oversee training and quality control	Verify professional credentials and experience with digitization, metadata creation, and quality control methodologies
Equipment	Level of specialized equipment needed to complete digitization work in a reasonable timeframe	Dependent on the capacity of an in-house lab or specialized unit	Verify quality and currency of equipment as referenced by professional standards

In-house digitization may be an important component of an institution's existing ecosystem or it may be a designated area of future development outlined in an institution's digital strategy. Either way, it is important to keep in mind that digital stewardship implies administrative accountability demonstrated through the implementation of a range of collections-management processes and a financial resource investment that should be commensurate to the scope and scale of the digital project.

Unless an organization has a large in-house digitization facility, lab, or unit, there are important reasons to include outsourcing considerations during the planning of any digitization project. While establishing in-house services may require a significant resource investment, outsourcing digitization requires an equal amount of care in choosing a well-qualified vendor. Most GLAM institutions will start to explore project planning through a request for proposal (RFP). Although not an exhaustive list, an RFP for any digitization project should address the following areas:

- security protocols, including environmental specifications for the digitization facility
- digitization equipment specifications and an outline of digitization workflows and associated professional standards
- quality control procedures and additional file processing methods, including optical character recognition (OCR) for documents, transcription services for handwritten documents and audio and AV files, as well as the process for color correction, tonal adjustments, and batch editing
- shipment or transport procedures and proof of insurance
- metadata template with specification of the format for the delivery of the metadata
- file format requirements; digitization specifications, including the number of preservation, access, or proxy files; and an estimate of the number and size of files for the completed project[19]

Since digital stewardship requires administrative accountability for the long-term care of assets that are curated or created by an institution, planning for digitization projects should include ongoing costs for digital preservation storage. Long-term storage costs for any digitization project should be part of the funding source requirements before a project is undertaken in-house or by a vendor. While storage for digitized textual assets may be sustainable for many GLAM institutions, digitization of AV and graphic material may require a significant resource investment for ongoing preservation costs. To offset these costs, digitization funding models may include:

- *acquisitions and digital preservation budgets*: integrating gradual costs for storage into existing budgetary funds relating to acquisition or preservation allotments

- *endowments and fundraising*: creating fundraising campaigns around digitization initiatives or developing projects as part of donor negotiations for collection acquisitions
- *digitization on-demand*: instituting in-house digitization services that include storage costs as part of reproduction fees for newly digitized analog content
- *access on-demand or pay-per-view*: requiring small fees to download digitized content, especially AV assets that are stored in archive-tier cloud storage

From Monograph Cataloging to Metadata Harvesting and Remediation

With the decline of analog archival processing units and the movement toward strategic mass digitization, cataloging or technical services has generally evolved and redefined their roles by focusing on metadata creation and remediation projects, as well as adopting cross-functional approaches to metadata ingest workflows in order to optimize discovery of "hidden" distinctive collections. Metadata quality control has become essential in building reliable and efficient approaches to these collaborative endeavors that extend across GLAM institutions. In this context, cataloging units have metamorphosed into teams that manage descriptive metadata across the institution. And, under a unified digital-preservation framework, these teams have taken on additional stewardship responsibilities, which include the creation of preservation metadata in the form of representative information (RI), including file format identification and technical registry information, as well as preservation descriptive information (PDI), which includes data elements for provenance, context, fixity, and access rights.[20]

Within the framework of integrated collections management, GLAM institutions are developing workflows for the purpose of streamlining the creation and augmentation of metadata as a "value-added" service with special considerations for enhanced use and reuse through linked data.[21] With the goal of ensuring consistent efforts in managing metadata crosswalks, the GLAM sector has adopted the Open Archives Initiative (OAI), which focuses on developing a framework where metadata can be harvested from multiple digital collections or repositories. In the context of the OAI, harvesting refers to the aggregation of metadata from a number of distributed repositories into a combined data store. The goal of the Open Archives Initiatives Protocol for Metadata Harvesting (OAI-PMH) is to supply and promote an application-independent interoperability framework that is used by a variety of communities who are engaged in publishing content on the web.[22] Although the OAI-PMH primarily focuses on enhancing the discoverability of published or open digital assets, its functional protocol, relating to interoperability and open access, can be applied to other internal systems, protocols, and workflows that support integrated collections management. Tenets of open access and interoperable metadata require that:

- metadata and metadata standards be part of a network
- metadata be open and reusable
- metadata benefits multiple, broad user communities
- metadata supports new research and digital scholarship methods
- metadata standards have active maintenance and governance structures
- metadata be extensible and embeddable
- metadata standards follow the rules of "graceful degradation" and "responsive design"[23]

One basic principle of integrative collections management is that any open digital asset should be accessible to all that need to find it and in a format that can be reused or remixed, so individuals do not have to re-create it. The OAI-PMH meets these criteria by requiring protocols that emphasize interoperable and scalable standards while ensuring reuse and value-added services, which provide opportunities for content providers or content stewards to add descriptive, technical, and rights-related metadata throughout the lifecycle management of any digital asset.[24]

Building Bridges: Research Data Management and Digital Archives

Similar to the emphasis on metadata harvesting, remediation, and reuse, research data management (RDM) and digital preservation communities both share the common goal of keeping research data accessible and usable. In many ways, RDM is a digital-stewardship activity that provides a type of archival value and, in theory, is a first step toward digital-preservation planning. RDM typically focuses on early lifecycle management of data by making researchers accountable for creating and maintaining well-documented data in a sustainable format. Guided by principles of integrated collections management, RDM policies should articulate the key stewardship activities involved in managing data from the initial planning phases to its curation and preservation.[25]

Challenges of RDM include insufficient metadata, missing information relating to provenance, and mismanagement of data early in its lifecycle. To mitigate these challenges, RDM combines digital-preservation and digital-archiving initiatives with the collaborative work of researchers, librarians, curators, and archivists who draw on core digital-stewardship concepts and conceptual models including the DCC Curation Lifecycle Model, the OAIS Functional Model, and FAIR and PREMIS metadata schemas. Stewards of research data face a large set of choices in developing archival and digital-preservation strategies that require the documentation of data formats and associated size, methods of file encryption and compression, storage media and durability, and approaches to data replication, distribution, verification, and repair. Many current RDA models and frameworks are available to bridge a range of archival functions early in the lifecycle management of research data to a set of preservation policies and "at-risk" profiles with the intention of managing the overall preservation costs for "big research data." Other digital-stewardship models for research data include rapid data appraisal methodology, as well as born-digital processes for identifying, intervening, and revitalizing data-rich material to produce preservation-ready assets.[26]

Acting Locally to Connect Globally: Diversifying Discovery Platforms

In addition to more proactive and collaborative approaches to research data management, integrated collections management takes into consideration the "environmental dynamism" of an ecosystem that arises from the interconnectedness of assets as global resources.[27] One of the primary goals of integrated collections management is the ability to leverage a DAME infrastructure and cross-functional workflows to enhance and diversify digital-service pathways with a focus on expanding global connections and enhanced discoverability. In the context of limited resources, integrated collections management empowers libraries, archives, and museums to contemplate more holistic infrastructures with an eye for regional consortia and digital-preservation federations to navigate the budgetary challenges that come with raising the visibility of local distinctive digital collections to expanded global communities. Broad cost benefits come from thinking internationally about library, archives, and museum collections. In the future, GLAM institutions will not only be measured by the size and quality of their digital collections but also on how they connect their distinctive digital ecosystems to a larger community of users. Building on the tradition of networked environments and linked data, integrated collections management positions more and more libraries, archives, and museums to engage with unified discovery platforms with the goal of highlighting interdisciplinary and transnational themes that will foster new global communities of engagement. In this context, the return on investment of this framework is based on one simple principle—integrated collections management can bring together materials that were once disparate into a single virtual space, accessible to anyone from anywhere.[28]

To support the success of this goal, integrated collections management is reliant on libraries', museums', and archives' continued advocacy for the open-access movement and the benefits that open content, open source, and open standards confer. As open access remains the foundation for digital repository development, it's critical that the GLAM sector continue to explore approaches for expanding these platforms to accommodate new forms of digital content, including diverse intellectual content, open educational resources, social media, time-based art work, rich media, and born-digital institutional records with a greater focus on a holistic integrated collections-management framework. In addition to moving digital content beyond an individual institutional repository, diversified discovery platforms and integrated collections-management workflows provide a greater focus on data analytics and data-mining, which can serve as an indicator of collection use and user behavior that will be an important foundation for informing a digital strategy and digital-stewardship budget decisions in the future.

Notes

1. Stacy Kowalczyk, *Digital Curation for Libraries and Archives* (Santa Barbara, CA: Libraries Unlimited, 2018), 110–11; Shailesh Kumar Shivakumar, *Enterprise Content and Search Management for Building Digital Platforms* (Hoboken, NJ: Wiley, 2016), 25.

2. Leslie Johnston, "Challenges in Preserving and Archiving Digital Materials," *Information Services and Use* 40, no. 3 (2020): 193–99, https://content.iospress.com/articles/information-services-and-use/isu200090.

3. Shivakumar, *Enterprise Content and Search Management*, 21.

4. Ibid., 24.

5. Ibid., 29–30.

6. Ross Spencer, "Digital Preservation as a Thought Experiment," in *Digital Preservation in Libraries: Preparing for a Sustainable Future*, eds. Jeremy Myntti and Jessalyn Zoom (Chicago: American Library Association, 2019), 27.

7. Elizabeth Yakel, "Digital Assets for the Next Millennium," *OCLC Systems and Services: International Digital Library Perspectives* 20, no. 3 (September 2004): 103.

8. Christine Madsen and Megan Hurst, "Digital Preservation Policy and Strategy," in *Digital Preservation in Libraries: Preparing for a Sustainable Future*, eds. Jeremy Myntti and Jessalyn Zoom (Chicago: American Library Association, 2019), 39.

9. Leslie Johnston, "Challenges in Preserving and Archiving Digital Materials"; Emily Rafferty and Becca Pad, "Better Together: A Holistic Approach to Creating a Digital Preservation Policy in an Art Museum," *Art Documentation: Bulletin of the Art Libraries Society of North America* 36 (Spring 2017): 149–62; Stephanie Hilles, "Building Alliances: Advocating for Art Methodologies in Digital Collections Collaborations," *Art Libraries Journal* 45 (April 2020): 73–77; Madsen and Hurst, "Digital Preservation Policy and Strategy," 39.

10. Lori J. Ashley, "Creating a Preservation Strategy," in *Building Trustworthy Digital Repositories: Theory and Implementation*, ed. Philip C. Bantin (New York: Rowman & Littlefield, 2016), 307–11.

11. Angela Fritz, "From Collection Silos to Digital Content Hubs: Digital Project Management in Special Collections and University Archives," in *Project Management in the Library Workplace (Advances in Library Administration and Organization, vol., 38)*, eds. Alice Daugherty and Samantha Schmehl Hines (Bingley, United Kingdom: Emerald Publishing, 2018), 190–92.

12. Vanessa A. Garofalo, "Doing Things Differently in the Cloud: Streamlining Library Workflows to Maximize Efficiency," *Proceedings of the Charleston Library Conference* (2014), accessed November 11, 2020, http://dx.doi.org/10.5703/1288284315591; Daniel Dollar, Gregory Eow, Julie Linden, and Melissa Grafe, "Distinctive Collections: The Space Between 'General' and 'Special' Collections and Implications for Collection Development," *Proceedings of the Charleston Library Conference* (2012), accessed November 11, 2020, http://dx.doi.org/10.5703/1288284315094; Michelle M. Wu, "Shared Collection Development, Digitization, and Owned Digital Collections," *Collection Management* 44, no. 2 (2019): 131–45.

13. Yakel, "Digital Assets for the Next Millennium," 104.

14. Elizabeth Ferguson Keathley, *Digital Asset Management: Content Architectures, Project Management, and Creating Order Out of Media Chaos* (Berkeley, CA: Apress, 2014), 57–58.

15. Katharine Schopflin, "Information Management Approaches to Digital Asset Management: A Case Study in Success and Failure," *Journal of Digital Media Management* 3, no. 4 (2015): 312.

16. Keathley, *Digital Asset Management*, 117–19.

17. Mark Walter, "Architectural Considerations in Digital Asset Management," *The Gilbane Report*, October 5, 2004, 4–5, accessed November 11, 2020, https://gilbane.com/wp-content/uploads/2020/01/GilbaneWP_StellentIBM_1.0.pdf.

18. Fritz, "From Collection Silos to Digital Content Hubs," 190–92.

19. Northeast Document Conservation Center, "Outsourcing and Vendor Relations," accessed November 11, 2020, https://www.nedcc.org/free-resources/preservation-leaflets/6.-reformatting/6.7-outsourcing-and-vendor-relations.

20. Linda R. Musser and Christopher H. Walker, "Cataloging for Collection Management," in *Rethinking Collection Development and Management*, eds. Becky Albitz, Christine Avery, and Diane Zabel (Santa Barbara, CA: Libraries Unlimited, 2014), 235; Junli Diao and Mirtha A, Hernandez, "Transferring Cataloging Legacies into Descriptive Metadata Creation in Digital Projects: Catalogers' Perspective," *Journal of Library Metadata* 14 (2014): 130–45; Sarah Buchanan, Elaine Franco, and John Sherlock, "Digging into our Hidden Collections: Maximizing Staff Skills and Technology to Enhance Access to Special Collections," ALCTS Affiliates Showcase, ALA Annual Conference, Anaheim, California, June 23, 2010, accessed November 11, 2020, http://carl-acrl.org/Archives/ConferencesArchive/Conference 10/2010proceedings/ElaineFranco.pdf; Michelle Flinchbaugh, "Biz of Acq/The Biz of Digital-Gone with the Old-In with the New-The Disappearance of Library Acquisitions and the Emergence of the E- and the Digital," *Against the Grain* 30, no. 2 (2018): 54–55.

21. Philip C. Bantin, "Creating and Capturing Metadata," in *Building Trustworthy Digital Repositories: Theory and Implementation*, ed. Philip C. Bantin (New York: Rowman & Littlefield, 2016), 119–23.

22. Shirpa Awasthi and Babita Jaiswal, "Open Archives Metadata Harvesting: An Overview," accessed November 11, 2020, http://ir.inflibnet.ac.in:8080/ir/bitstream/1944/1130/1/15.pdf.

23. Kowalczyk, *Digital Curation for Libraries and Archives*, 123–24.

24. Marshall Breeding, "Understanding the Protocol for Metadata Harvesting of the Open Archives Initiative," *Computers in Library* 22, no. 8 (September 2002): 24–29.

25. Michelle Lindlar, Pia Rudnik, Sarah Jones, and Laurence Horton, "You Say Potato, I Say Potato: Mapping Digital Preservation and Research Data Management Concepts toward Collective Curation and Preservation Strategies," *International Journal of Digital Curation* 15, no. 1 (2020): 2–4.

26. See Jake Carlson, "The Data Curation Profiles Toolkit: The Profile Template," paper 4, November 29, 2010, accessed November 11, 2020, http://dx.doi.org/10.5703/1288284315653; Cooper T. Clarke and Hilary Szu Yin Shiue, "Data Rescue Processing Guide: A Practical Guide to Processing Preservation Ready Data from Research Data Collections," National Agricultural Library of U.S. Department of Agriculture, August 2020, accessed November 11, 2020, https://drum.lib.umd.edu/bitstream/handle/1903/26473/ClarkeShiue_DataRescueProcessingGuide.pdf?sequence=1&isAllowed=y; Micah Altman and Richard Landau, "Selecting Efficient and Reliable Preservation Strategies: Modelling Long-Term Information Integrity Using the Large-Scale Hierarchical Discrete Event Simulator," *International Journal of Digital Curation* 15, no. 1 (2020): 1–18.

27. Adrian Yeow, Christina Soh, and Rina Hansen, "Aligning with a New Digital Strategy: A Dynamic Capabilities Approach," *Journal of Strategic Information Systems*, 27 (2018): 44–45.

28. Lisa Carter and Beth Whittacker, "Area Studies and Special Collections: Shared Challenges, Shared Strengths," *Libraries and the Academy* 15, no. 2 (April 2015): 353–73.

CHAPTER FIVE

Cloud-Based Digital-Preservation Storage

A Building Block for Sustainable Digital Stewardship

While digital stewardship encompasses many components, digital-preservation storage is the essential building block for the sustainability and growth of any DAME. As part of an enterprise digital strategy, a storage model should be informed by collection needs, as well as an understanding of basic storage infrastructure. Since storage costs are the greatest expenditure for managing and maintaining a digital-asset management ecosystem, strategies should be guided by flexible approaches to allow institutions the ability to "pivot" as new storage solutions evolve. The emergence of cloud-based storage offers libraries, museums, and archives a sustainable option for long-term storage that not only supports a distributed digital-preservation model based on geographic replication but also facilitates tier-based approaches to ensure storage diversification at reduced costs. This chapter provides an overview of digital-preservation storage technologies, practices, requirements, strategies, and cost models to ensure sustainable solutions for the long-term care and accessibility of unique digital assets managed by museums, libraries, and archives.

Defining Digital-Preservation Storage Requirements

Storage options for any DAME will change with evolving technologies, the increased volume and expanding file size of digital assets, and the ever-changing cloud storage marketplace.[1] Since storage requirements for digital assets are quite stringent, it is important to review best practices and standards before deciding on any storage device, system, or service provider. Although these standards are not entirely comprehensive, the following criteria and conceptual models provide a good overview of some of the basic requirements for digital preservation storage:

- **The OAIS Reference Model** defines the archival storage function for a digital archives system, provides guidelines for maintaining and retrieving archival information packages (AIP), outlines storage paths for assets, and describes the process of managing fixity checks essential for monitoring the health of assets after they have been deposited into a storage environment.
- **The NDSA Levels of Preservation** outlines functional requirements for digital-preservation storage, including recommendations relating to data redundancy, geographically dispersed storage locations, documentation requirements, and guidance on data integrity and access controls.
- **The Trustworthy Repositories Audit and Certification (TRAC) Criteria and Checklist** provides a listing of technological requirements that relate to assessing the trustworthiness of a digital archiving system including storage environments. The core principles of the criteria focus on documentation, transparency, adequacy, and measurability.
- **The ISO/IEC 27000 Series** provides highly referenced information security standards for digital storage. Specifically, ISO 27040:2015 focuses on data-storage systems and infrastructure, risk assessment, and information security controls to improve quality assurance and audits trails in order to protect stored data.

Characteristics of a Digital-Preservation Storage Environment

As outlined by these best practices and standards, digital-preservation storage is a delicate ecosystem that not only ensures data integrity but also safeguards the long-term health of assets in a closely monitored environment. Similar to analog or print-based collections that are housed in carefully monitored physical collection facilities, storage for digital assets requires a specific controlled environment that ensures a safe, trusted, and protected digital storage space. Regardless of the type, or combination of types, of storage used, it is important to understand the distinguishing characteristics of a digital-preservation storage environment, as well as how these spaces differ from other types of digital storage.[2] Characteristics of a digital-preservation environment include:

- *Redundancy* refers to the preservation of multiple copies of any one digital asset. Redundancy can be integrated into workflows as part of a broad storage path, which may also include the automated replication of data from one primary storage location to several other locations.
- *Geographic replication* is based on the best practice of maintaining three copies of any asset, stored on two different storage media, in at least one geographically disparate location. Replication in independent cloud-based storage locations may vary from different geographic locations in one country to storage locations in different countries.
- *Checksums creation and fixity verification* enable the creation of a unique footprint or "checksum" for each digital asset that enters a digital-storage environment. Checksums are maintained as a distinct algorithm and are used to detect changes to data files that reside in a storage environment. Changes to checksums are ascertained through fixity verification that may signal that further file review or file repair is needed. Fixity checks can only reveal that a file has been changed. Fixity verification does not indicate what aspect of the file has been altered.
- *Audit trails* are logs that document data integrity and fixity discrepancies. Adding an essential layer of security, audit trails document approved users and internet protocol (IP) addresses that have accessed data within a digital-preservation storage environment. Audit logs provide essential documentation that may reveal information pertaining to inadvertent asset release, malicious attacks, and cyber threats.
- *Integrity monitoring* is the scheduled review of various aspects of the storage configuration and environment, including hardware checks, activity documentation, and data-integrity verification. Integrity monitoring can range from tracking file size and file counts at a high level to more in-depth tracking and verification of checksums at the asset-level. Systematic storage monitoring can be scheduled on a daily, weekly, monthly, or yearly basis.
- *Access controls* include a range of activities that limit access to a digital-preservation storage environment. Access controls include managing and closely monitoring the roles and permissions of groups of users and individuals, as well as instituting two-way authentication. Within a digital-preservation environment, any access control should also enable diversification among a limited group of users to ensure that no one person has access to all the copies of stored data.

It is important to note that digital-preservation storage is not the same thing as a "back-up," which is used for recovering data for emergency-response purposes. Back-ups are static copies of data made for disaster recovery; they do not serve as an authentic replicated copy of the data in the context of digital-preservation best practices.[3] Back-up copies are managed in consultation with IT departments and ensure the original data or a version of the original data can be restored due to hardware, software, or media failure; a natural disaster; or malicious actions. Back-up copies are usually scheduled on a regular basis and are often overwritten within a designated time period of weeks or months.[4] Although back-ups are essential for continuity of business operations, they do not meet the requirements of a full replication strategy suitable for a preservation storage environment.[5]

Storage Architecture

In addition to the special characteristics of digital-preservation storage, it is also important to understand the different ways that storage systems are structured and organized, more commonly referred to as a storage architecture. A storage architecture is comprised of a network that transfers data between different types of storage devices, servers, or service providers. Within a digital-preservation environment, storage architectures tend to be organized by "latency," which refers to the time it takes to transfer data from a storage location to the end user. Storage architecture affects how fast data can be accessed based on a range of solutions, organized hierarchically from low latency to high latency.[6] Types of storage architecture include:

- *Online storage*, which facilitates frequent access, is defined by fast retrieval speeds and ease of use for ready availability of data. Cloud storage is a type of online storage that can be purchased through a third-party service as an alternative to traditional offline storage. Online storage can be scaled to a network enterprise model for digital-asset storage. Because of its low latency, online storage tends to be the most expensive type of storage architecture.
- Data maintained in *nearline storage* tends to be slower to retrieve than online storage, as it is maintained external to a computer. Retrieval of assets is usually controlled by a storage-management system, which facilitates quick and scalable access to data. There are a variety of approaches to nearline storage. An LTO (linear tape-open) tape library system is a common type of nearline storage that manages large volumes of data on magnetic tape cartridges, stored as part of a robotic

tape library. Like most nearline options, tape storage may have higher latency than online storage, be difficult and expensive to upgrade, and require a greater need for environmental controls and security monitoring within the data center that houses the LTO library. Depending on the nature of the storage system, nearline storage is moderately priced.
- *Offline storage* manages data on a specific medium or external device. Since these storage devices can be easily transported, offline storage is characterized by its portability, as well as a high latency and high risk of media deterioration or failure. Offline storage represents the least expensive type of storage.

Traditionally, many libraries, archives, and museums have used a combination of different storage types in order to ensure data redundancy at a low cost. For example, low-resolution access copies that are small in size may reside on online storage while high-resolution digital-preservation copies may reside on nearline or offline storage or a combination of both. Some institutions may have integrated direct attached storage (DAS) as a solution to improve latency levels at reduced costs. For others, networked attached storage (NAS) is a strategy that has been adopted to manage large amounts of rich-media assets, while others have built a storage architecture network (SAN) that attaches remote devices in such a way that the devices appear locally attached to servers. Each of these storage solutions has built in redundancy to safeguard against hard drive failure.[7] A RAID storage subsystem is a redundant array of independent disks that use parity as way to protect data in case one of the hard drives fail. It is important to note that hard drives or tape drives are not considered appropriate for long-term storage without significant monitoring and migration plans to mitigate the risk of tape deterioration.[8] Although nearline and offline represent feasible storage options for most GLAM institutions, the downside of organizations managing their own storage architecture includes staff reduction and turnover as well as the resource investment required for maintenance and upgrades, implementing and updating information security protocols, and managing the synchronization of versioning between back-up copies.[9]

Overview of Cloud-Based Storage

Although tape storage has provided the primary storage media for libraries, museums, and archives in the past, GLAM communities are gravitating to the cloud for their future storage needs. Cloud storage is a model of networked online storage where data is maintained in virtualized pools hosted by third-party providers. Cloud storage allows institutions to send data from their local systems to the cloud, which provides on-demand access to a shared pool of configurable computing resources such as application servers, storage servers, and networks. Cloud-based storage can be quickly implemented with minimal management on the users' end, and computing services can be paid according to a "pay-as-you-go" price model.[10] Open APIs facilitate access to cloud-based services, and, at the same time, facilitate the integration of these services with other applications and solutions that may be used as components or building blocks for a larger digital-asset management ecosystem.[11]

The National Institute of Standards and Technology (NIST) defines the following five essential characteristics of cloud computing:

- *On demand self-service* provides users with automatic access to storage resources based on their specific needs without interaction with the service provider.
- *Broad network access* facilitates computing capabilities over the network by standardized protocols so that any kind of client platform may access the services as long as users have access to the network.
- *Resource pooling* enables the aggregation of storage resources in order to serve multiple users. Multitenant architectures allow different data producers to share the same storage application while safeguarding access controls for each tenant.[12] It is important to note that assets in multitenant, cloud-computing environments are dynamically assigned and reassigned to fulfill the demands of cloud-based tenants, which means that the user has no control of the exact location of their digital assets.[13]
- *Rapid elasticity* facilitates quick expansion of access capabilities based on demands and future needs. From the users' perspective, the storage resources are "virtually unlimited" and can be provisioned at any quantity at any time.
- *Measured service* means that usage is monitored, controlled, and reported, which provides transparency about the amount of storage that is in use for both the service provider and the data owner.[14]

These defining characteristics are meant to provide a baseline to compare cloud-based options with alternative storage architectures, as well as to assist institutions in developing cost-effective, diversified storage strategies. In addition, the essential characteristics of cloud computing support three cloud-based service models.[15] These service layers include:

- *Cloud software-as-a-service* (*SaaS*) gives institutions use of software from providers that are run on a cloud infrastructure. SaaS provides all the necessary underlying infrastructure and platforms to run applications and pricing is on a pay-as-you-go use basis or a subscription fee.
- *Cloud platform-as-a-service* (*PaaS*) offers a variety of types of environments for application development, ranging from operating systems to program-language execution environments, to databases, to web-servers, to data-management solutions.
- *Cloud infrastructure-as-a-service* (*IaaS*) encompasses virtual machines, storage services, and network services. IaaS does not allow for the management of an underlying cloud infrastructure but provides access to operating systems and storage, as well as limited control over given resources like a firewall.

In addition to advantages such as connectivity, network access, and data distribution, cloud storage can provide a comparably low-cost, scalable platform for storing data within a digital-preservation environment. Deployment models, which refer to the way that cloud systems are implemented, can either be deployed internally (on-premise) or externally (off-premise) and are summarized by the NIST definition as follows:

- *Private cloud* is operated (or leased) exclusively by an enterprise or institution, managed internally or by a third-party or both. Private enterprise cloud is often dedicated to and operated by a single institution or data producer. As the most expensive type of deployment, the private cloud is important for institutions who place a high degree of importance on information security and the protection of confidential information and proprietary data.[16]
- *Public cloud* is offered to the public via a large-scale infrastructure and often operates over non-trusted networks.
- *Community cloud* is based on a shared infrastructure designed for a designated community who may be united by geography, common concerns, missions, content, or asset type. Community clouds may be managed internally or by a third-party and either hosted on- or off-premise. The costs for the storage infrastructure are shared by the members of the community.
- *Hybrid cloud* is a composition of two or more types of cloud deployments described above. The hybrid cloud offers the benefits of a multiple deployment model, capitalizing on storage capacity or capabilities by

aggregating and integrating with another service in order to customize or extend cloud-based storage options.[17]

Different cloud deployments models offer varying "economies of scale" by expanding or reducing storage capacity and pooling institution-wide resources in a way that encourages flexibility and cost savings.[18] For example, many GLAM communities are formulating digital-preservation federations with the goal of building a hybrid, distributed digital-preservation storage network that enables its members to securely cache and preserve content in geographically dispersed storage sites. More and more of these federations are investing in distributed cloud-based storage protocols that prevent data loss or corruption, while avoiding the initial investment of expensive infrastructure setup, large equipment replacement, and daily maintenance and upgrade costs.[19] These institutions are turning to the cloud for their individualized storage needs, which can be met through a mixture of internally and externally managed, layered storage in hybrid models. These distributed models are based on a tiered strategy that ensures both flexibility and diversification through multiple storage layers that support geographic replication, information security protocols, and access controls for a trusted digital-preservation environment.[20]

Tiered-Storage Strategies

The objective of multi-tiered storage is to create a single consolidated strategy around all levels of cloud services provided by either a single or multiple cloud providers. To accommodate this model, each cloud provider offers individual tiers of storage that have different performance, access, and pricing levels. By devising tier-based strategies, institutions can assign different types of data to various layers, partitions, or shares on cloud storage with the object of reducing total storage costs. A tiered storage architecture places data in a hierarchy, prioritized on performance, costs, and volume or capacity. In this context, storage strategies are flexible and meet the varying needs of GLAM institutions based on a whole host of factors, including total volume and average file size; estimated growth; anticipated use; speed for access or data latency; historic significance; business, legal, and administrative value; research or records management compliance requirements; and access, privacy, confidentiality, copyright, or license restrictions. These tiers include:

- *Tier 1 (Hot Data) (Performance or Access Proxy)* is designed for active content for immediate, frequent use. This tier offers the lowest activity costs, lowest latency, and the highest pricing.
- *Tier 2 (Warm Data) (Low Touch or Access Master)* is considered a "low-touch" tier for ready access to mostly semi-active or inactive data. Low-touch tiers offer availability and low latency retrieval times with lower storage costs. Activity costs are higher than the performance of high-access tiers.
- *Tier 3 (Cool Data) (Archival or Digital-Preservation Master)* is considered an archive tier. Ideal for digital-preservation masters, retrieval times are not immediate and data owners can sometimes wait for hours or days for retrieval of assets. Archive tiers are geared toward assets that are unlikely to require immediate access but do require long-term retention. The overall storage costs are low on this tier with the tradeoff of the slowest retrieval response time. In addition, archive storage tiers may have usage fees to recall assets that can nullify the low pricing structure.
- *Tier 4 (Cold Data) (Deep or Dark Archival Storage)* represents cold or dark storage, used for long-term retention of assets that are rarely accessed. It is important to note that for some storage providers, Tier 1 may be made of solid-state drives and successive archival tiered levels may involve RAID systems, tape offline systems, and cloud-based nearline or offline storage systems, which may constitute much longer retrieval times.

Tiered storage models may include five or more tiered storage levels, each providing different combinations of basic storage attributes.[21] The more tiers

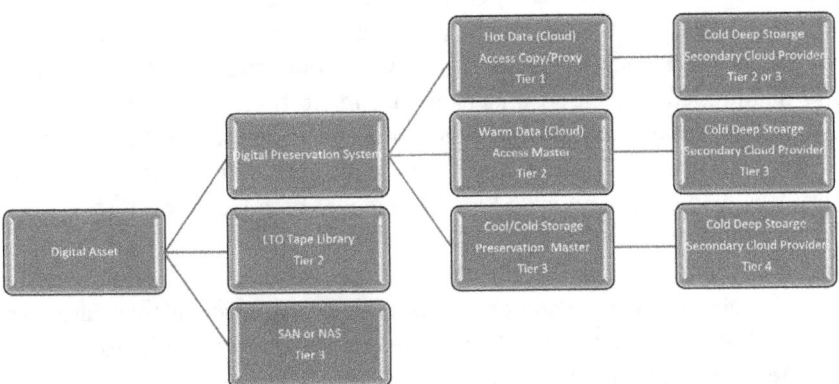

Figure 5.1. Example of a Tiered-Based Storage Strategy

that are available, the more efficient data can be stored to meet the performance and budgetary needs of institutions at an enterprise level. Libraries, museums, and archives can anticipate that providers will release additional variations and options for tiered storage over time. For example, many proprietary digital-preservation systems already are moving toward providing a comprehensive digital-preservation environment complete with a full suite of services, including tiered-storage options using the SaaS model. In this context, tiered storage builds in all of the requirements necessary for a digital-preservation environment while allowing institutions the flexibility to decide, at the asset or collection level, the number of copies of each digital asset that are kept, as well as where each asset is stored. As storage layers expand and diversify, many institutions will abandon on-premise solutions for select multi-cloud providers as part of a multi-tiered cloud strategy. By selecting data centers from different providers, organizations can mitigate single-point failure and continuity risks from a sole storage infrastructure service.[22]

Considerations for Secure Cloud Storage

Despite the many advantages, cloud storage also introduces new security challenges for GLAM institutions. The two major concerns include safeguarding data integrity and ensuring controls to prohibit unauthorized access.[23] Cloud data security has multiple layers of risk that arise with the transfer of data. The movement of data complicates the process of securing it, as it must be protected at the point of origin, the point of receipt, on the device that transmits it, on the device that receives it, and at all times when it is in transit.[24] Before investing in a cloud option, institutions should understand the provider's security model and ask to review the way storage services are offered and organized. Additionally, security vulnerabilities arise through network endpoints and with network connections that are managed and maintained locally, so understanding institutional data handling and in-house storage security protocols is equally important. Regardless of where data resides, it is important to understand that there are risks associated with both locally managed and cloud-based storage.[25] Broad areas of storage security requirements include:

- *The ability to secure data content* refers to safety protocols that safeguard authorized restrictions to data access, specifically as it relates to the protection of confidential and sensitive data and proprietary information. In the cloud environment, digital assets are out of the direct control

of owners, so providers must allow assurances that data is not made available or disclosed to unauthorized users. To ensure protection, sensitive data should be encrypted in motion and at rest. Encrypting data before storing it in the cloud allows institutions the ability to protect the data as the data owners control encryption keys and passwords. In addition to controlling and managing encryption keys, data should only be decrypted within the boundaries of the data owner's organization.[26]
- *The ability to safeguard data integrity* refers to the information security protocols that ensure protection against improper data modification or destruction, as well as protection of data authenticity, accuracy, and completeness. Specific data-handling and auditing protocols protect the data from unauthorized changes, disclosure, and deletion. Data in the cloud has to be stored correctly and in a trustworthy preservation environment that is monitored on a regular basis.
- *The ability to control access to data* refers to security protocols that ensure only authenticated users have access to data. Storage services should grant GLAM institutions the ability to set up granular levels of access to individuals and specific groups of users. Additionally, network security needs to be in place and include password protection, two-step authentication, firewall implementation and monitoring, deployment of virus detection software, and the use of confidentiality agreements among employees who have access to the data.[27] Access protocols should also be organized around "the principle of least privilege," which refers to coordinating users' work processes to the lowest level of access, read/write, and execution rights associated with their work roles as outlined in their position descriptions. In addition, cloud service should provide documentation on processes for data recovery and response protocols for a data breach.[28]

Cloud hosting presents additional challenges for libraries, museums, and archives as institutions navigate where cloud servers are geographically located as well as address information governance questions relating to who "owns" data (as well as associated metadata) in the cloud and how it will be protected.[29] Object storage, the central model for cloud providers, is based on large-scale data repositories designed to cover wide geographies, both within and outside the country. Cloud service providers operate large data centers, which they may own, lease, or rent.[30] Since laws regarding privacy, copyright, and security can vary significantly from country to country, cloud service providers need to be transparent in detailing where data is located, as well as how they protect data owners' privacy and data security. For any cloud service provider, the service level agreement (SLA) outlines the terms for cloud services, which will include how data is stored and retrieved, as well as where data is stored.[31]

Storage Pricing and Cost Models

Although the preservation of physical library, museum, and archival collections continues to remain an issue, more and more GLAM institutions have embraced multi-institutional, high-density storage facilities as a solution to alleviate space management concerns. Virtual space poses equally as pressing concerns for the GLAM community whose "digital mortgage" of assets require the same consideration of virtual space management, whether it is locally managed, in cloud-based storage, or in "dark archives" in geographically dispersed data grids across the country.[32] In order to estimate long-range financial planning for digital storage, it is important to have a reasonable estimate of costs. While cloud storage offerings by leading companies have similar price models, the future of the cloud-based marketplace will become more competitive. With the evolving nature of cloud-based storage services, it is important to keep the following cloud storage pricing variables in mind:

- *Capacity* extends to an institution's current data volume and anticipated growth. In developing a storage cost model, it is extremely important to understand institutional data, holistically. Revisiting the latest institution-wide digital-stewardship assessment provides an essential snapshot of the ecosystem including format variations, estimated size, anticipated use and value, as well as access and copyright restrictions. It is important to keep in mind that some storage providers may offer discount volume prices for cloud-based access or archive storage tiers. In this scenario, monthly costs may decrease as the data volume reaches certain thresholds. In other instances, charges may be prorated so customers are charged for capacity consumed over time, and in other instances, service providers offer a "pay-as-you-go" model.
- *Storage operations and data transactions* include activities such as writing, reading, and data retrieval. In many instances, data transfer and retrieval in a cloud-based environment may have associated fees. In general, costs are not high unless data is being transferred in between data centers in different geographic regions. Additionally, snapshots and backups can significantly increase storage costs and network charges. Some storage providers have developed a workaround for the high cost of geo-redundant storage replication with the "snowball," a

physical device, similar to a large external hard drive, used to transfer large amounts of data in and out of the cloud. While some providers may have data transport solutions similar to the snowball, others may require network transfers based on data volume, which will be outlined in the service contract.
- *Redundancy levels* required for digital-preservation storage can be an added source of "storage budget bloat." As a result, levels of replication requirements designated in preservation policies and best practices need careful consideration. While three copies of a PDF or a .tiff file may be affordable due to its small size, three copies of a high-definition digital video may not be a sustainable redundancy strategy for most institutions.

Hidden Costs: Egress Charges and Exit Strategies

It is important to note that cloud storage pricing does not always cost less than an on-premise option. Hidden cloud-storage costs can add up. One of the most substantive hidden costs is egress charges. Although many cloud providers do not charge for ingesting data into the cloud, many providers institute charges for data retrieval. The two types of egress charges include retrieving data from storage and downloading data from a storage tier.[33] Both charges can make cloud storage very expensive. These charges vary from provider to provider and are largely based on the amount of data moved and the geographic location where the data resides. In addition, egress charges can be sizable if an institution:

- is switching from one cloud storage provider to another
- is adopting a multi-cloud strategy
- is requiring a cross-regional transfer
- is requiring a large-scale litigation hold as a result of e-discovery
- is frequently accessing archived data in cold or dark storage layers[34]

Selection of a cloud-storage provider also encompasses investing in the financial future of the provider as well as the long-term maintenance, development, and upgrades of the provider's storage architecture. Risks that relate to service changes, price increases, or the financial dissolution of the service provider may require institutions to migrate their assets to another service. Reviewing a documented exit strategy is an important part of negotiating storage-related contracts and service agreements, as well as consortia memberships. Exit strategies should outline a migration plan and include a data inventory, the mapping of any data dependencies, an overview of bulk export functions, the inclusion of log files and AIPs accessibility, and the ability to engage in test migrations. Some proprietary companies may provide source code in escrow if they go out of business, thereby making migration paths available to their clients as they navigate next-generation storage solutions.[35]

Digital Stewardship and Sustainability: Looking to the Future

Beyond the evolving cloud-provider marketplace, the GLAM sector's responsiveness to the technological changes over the past decade are reflected in their evolving public and research services, their growing digital initiatives, and their ability to keep pace with the ever-growing information landscape, as well as the technical infrastructure required to support and sustain it. In this constantly expanding environment, the relevancy of any library, museum, or archive is measured by its ability to act on a jointly shared vision that meets the transformational goals and strategic needs of the institution. To accommodate this vision, libraries, museums, and archives are shifting away from a traditional service-orientation based on highly mediated, transactional encounters and instead are embracing public services and instructional programs that inspire one-to-one partnerships in learning defined by collaborations, curriculum development, and digital engagement. Increasingly, the GLAM sector is often seen as an "extension of the classroom" and envisions engagement as an ongoing conversation reliant on building and achieving lifelong learning objectives that are focused on critical thinking, creative engagement, and global perspectives.

Digital stewardship is critical in how libraries, museums, and archives are repositioning themselves to facilitate this new vision. As the landscape changes, efforts of librarians, archivists, and museum curators to manage digital content will continue to evolve with the shared values and mission of their institutions to guide their paths. As this book has shown, there is no one solution, tool, or individual that can manage the scope and scale of the future challenges relating to digital content; rather, collaborations with GLAM stakeholders within institutions and beyond will be the key to craft flexible strategies for the unique needs of their digital collections, as well as their diverse audiences. As innovative technologies and reimagined GLAM spaces empower the public to not only connect with but also curate and create knowledge, the future strategies and approaches to digital stewardship will constantly evolve with the learning, research, and public engagement needs of communities whose expectations are framed by emerging technologies in an information rich environment.

In many ways, changing approaches to collections management and related storage strategies serve as defining moments for GLAM institutions to accelerate their own transformations through collaborative action and innovative digital services. As libraries, museums, and archives become critical partners in managing an enterprise ecosystem of digital assets, sustainability becomes a greater concern. In this context, sustainability is meant to ensure the continuity and long-term accessibility of digital assets within reasonable management resource levels. Digital-stewardship sustainability is a long-term investment maintained by an institution-wide technological infrastructure that is necessary to make digital collections, research data, and institutional assets available over time. With a greater focus on holistic digital asset stewardship, collaborative institutional partnerships with chief information officers (CIOs) are critical in making strategic macro-decisions that are crucial in building a cost-effective storage infrastructure that is interoperable and scalable for future development.[36]

It is important to note that there is no one perfect solution for enterprise management of digital assets; rather, the challenge is an ever-evolving effort to keep up with an organization's current needs while, at the same time, continuing to plan for future circumstances. Unlike their analog counterparts, digital assets need constant monitoring and intervention to remain usable and authentic. In this sense, digital stewardship is an iterative process of continuous assessment, policy development, implementation, and maintenance. In this context, it is imperative that GLAM sector leadership establish a vision and implement a digital strategy that creates a culture of critical competencies—collaboration, problem solving, technological proficiency, and global awareness, as well as a commitment for purposeful uses of technology, meaningful professional development, and innovative cost modeling. In this way, looking toward the future becomes a positive process focused on creating a vision of what might be possible, which helps define the steps that can be taken to proactively move forward. With a digital-stewardship framework as a roadmap, the future for the GLAM sector will be built on a solid base that can be scalable to a social-networked world where data, knowledge, history, and cultural heritage can be accumulated, accessed, and reused in the personal spaces of tomorrow's diverse audiences.

Notes

1. Elizabeth Ferguson Keathley, *Digital Asset Management: Content Architectures, Project Management, and Creating Order Out of Media Chaos* (Berkeley, CA: Apress, 2014), 31.

2. Erin O'Meara and Kate Stratton, *Digital Preservation Storage: Trends in Archives Practice* (Chicago: Society of American Archivists, 2016), 4, 6–7.

3. Ibid., 4.

4. Gillian Oliver and Ross Harvey, *Digital Curation* (Chicago: Neal-Schuman, 2016), 185.

5. O'Meara and Stratton, *Digital Preservation Storage*, 4.

6. Yaniv Romem and Tom Leyden, "A Cloud Storage Architecture for the Enterprise," *InfoWorld*, May 24, 2017, https://www.infoworld.com/article/3198084/a-cloud-storage-architecture-for-the-enterprise.html.

7. Keathley, *Digital Asset Management*, 32–33; O'Meara and Stratton, *Digital Preservation Storage*, 10.

8. O'Meara and Stratton, *Digital Preservation Storage*, 5.

9. Edward M. Corrado and Heather Moulaison Sandy, *Digital Preservation for Libraries, Archives, and Museums* (Lanham, MD: Rowman & Littlefield, 2017), 151.

10. Tatiana Galibus, Viktor V. Krasnoproshin, Robson de Oliverira Albuquerque, and Edison Pignaton de Freitas, *Elements of Cloud Storage Security: Elements, Concepts, and Optimized Practices* (Cham, Switzerland: Springer Publishing, 2016), 2.

11. Ibid.

12. Aaron Wheeler and Michael Winburn, *Cloud Storage Security: A Practical Guide* (Waltham, MA: Elsevier Publishing, 2015), 5.

13. Galibus et al., *Elements of Cloud Storage Security*, 2.

14. Robert Smallwood, *Information Governance: Concepts, Strategies, and Best Practices* (Hoboken, NJ: Wiley, 2014), 288.

15. Galibus et al., *Elements of Cloud Storage Security*, 3.

16. Smallwood, *Information Governance*, 289.

17. Galibus et al., *Elements of Cloud Storage Security*, 7.

18. Smallwood, *Information Governance*, 285; Patricia C. Franks, *Records and Information Management* (Chicago: American Library Association, 2013), 161.

19. Kan Yang and Xiaohua Jia, *Security for Cloud Storage Systems* (Cham, Switzerland: Springer Publishing, 2013), 2; Galibus et al., *Elements of Cloud Storage Security*, 5, 8.

20. Corrado and Sandy, *Digital Preservation for Libraries*, 172.

21. Zouheir Daher and Hassen Hajjdiab, "Cloud Storage Comparative Analysis Amazon Simple Storage vs. Microsoft Azure Blob Storage," *International Journal of Machine Learning and Computing* 8, no. 1 (February 2018): 85–86.

22. Ibid., 33, 155.

23. Yang and Jia, *Security for Cloud Storage Systems*, 2.

24. Wheeler and Winburn, *Cloud Storage Security*, 4, 10.

25. Smallwood, *Information Governance*, 293.

26. Wheeler and Winburn, *Cloud Storage Security*, 18, 101, 115.

27. Oliver and Harvey, *Digital Curation*, 187–88.

28. Wheeler and Winburn, *Cloud Storage Security*, 116.

29. Corrado and Sandy, *Digital Preservation for Libraries*, 172.

30. Yang and Jia, *Security for Cloud Storage Systems*, 2.
31. Wheeler and Winburn, *Cloud Storage Security*, 16.
32. Oliver and Harvey, *Digital Curation*, 179–80; O'Meara and Stratton, *Digital Preservation Storage*, 8.
33. Daher and Hajjdiab, "Cloud Storage Comparative Analysis," 87–88.
34. Ibid.
35. Corrado and Sandy, *Digital Preservation for Libraries*, 121.
36. Robert D. Montoya, "Advocating for Sustainability: Scaling Down Library Digital Infrastructure," *Journal of Library Administration* 56, no. 5 (2016): 603–20.

Index

academic libraries: collection-management services for, 2; personnel in, 42–43
access controls, 73
administration: in digital stewardship, 10–11; NARA as, 3–4
advocacy: digital stewardship and, 45, 46; IG and, 12–15; for open access, 66
AIP. See archival information packages
American Library Association (ALA), 4
analog collections: digital collections vs., xi–xii, xv, 2, 29, 37, 40–42; digitization of, 58–63, 60–61
application programming interfaces (API): in cloud-based services, 76; in interoperability, 38–39; as IR tool, 5, 21
archival information packages (AIP), 72, 84
archives: in integrated collections management, 64–65; management of, 58–59; NARA for, 3–4; OAIS in, 4, 25–26, 63–64, 72. See also galleries, libraries, archives and museums

assessment. See data assessment analysis models; digital stewardship assessment
assessment report, 31–32
assessment segmentation, 22, 22–25
audit trails, 73

back-up, digital preservation vs., 74
bibliographic data, 2–3
Borgman, Christine, 2

CAD. See computer-aided design
cataloging: as ILS, 2; in integrative collections management, 63–64
CCSDS. See Consultative Committee for Space Data Systems
checksum, 73
chief information officer (CIO), 85
cloud-based digital preservation storage: application programming interfaces in, 76; architecture of, 74–75; costs in, 29, 76, 82–84; deployment models of, 77–78; environmental characteristics of, 72–74; management in, 38–39; overview of,

75–78; security in, 80–83; service models of, 76–77; SLA for, 82; storage requirements defined, 71–72; tier-based strategies in, *xiii*, 78–80, 79. *See also* digital preservation
cloud computing, 76
cloud hosting, 81–82
collection-management system, 2–3, 52–53. *See also* analog collections; digital collections; integrative collections management; primary collection analysis
collection silo, 11, 20, 41–42
computer-aided design (CAD), 6
Consultative Committee for Space Data Systems (CCSDS), 4
CoreTrustSeal, 27
cost modeling: in cloud-based storage, 82–84; in digital stewardship, 29–30; as pay-as-you-go, 76, 82
cross-functional workflows: curation ready assets and, 56–58, 57; as integrative collections management, 55
curators. *See* subject curators

DAM. *See* digital assets management
DAME. *See* digital-asset management ecosystem
DAS. *See* direct attached storage
data: bibliographic, 2–3; forms of, 79, 79; security of, 80–81; as unstructured, 28–30
data assessment analysis models, 25–27
data curation: in digital stewardship, xii–xiv, 1, 3, 9; function of, 8; skills in, 45; transition in, 42–43
data research: CoreTrustSeal in, 27; in integrative collections management, 64–65
Data Seal of Approval (DSA), 27
DCC. *See* Digital Curation Centre's Data Curation Lifecycle Model
digital advocacy, 12–15, 45, 46, 66

digital asset: assessment scope and scale of, 19; centralization as value, 14; collection restructuring of, 37; cost associated with, 29; cross-functional workflows, curation ready assets and, 56–58, 57; ecosystem of, 6–8, 7; environment characteristics of, 73
digital asset inventory, 22, 24–25
digital-asset management ecosystem (DAME), xii, 1, 19; analysis and prioritized recommendations of, 30–31; assessment in, 21–27, 22, 31–32; assets in, 7, 7; cloud-based digital preservation in, 71–84; cost modeling for, 29–30; cross-functional workflows in, 56–58, 57; digital rights management in, 8, 13; digitization path in, 60–61, 60–63; distributed service architecture base of, 1, 37; GLAM in, xi, 12–15, 45, 46, 66; history of, 2–6; in institutions, xii–xv; IRs in, 4–5; IT, collections-management and, 52–53; master data management in, 5; multi-method approach to, 20–22; risk-management assessment for, 28; scale of, xii–xiv, 1; storage costs in, 76, 82–84; uniformity of stewardship in, 5, 11; unstructured data in, 28–30
digital assets management (DAM), 38
digital collection mapping, 22, 24
digital collections: analog collections vs., xi–xii, xv, 2, 29, 37, 40–42; of GLAM, xi–xiii, 1; management of, 19–20; primary analysis of, 23–24; silo reductions in, 11, 20, 41–42; strategy for, 37; technical infrastructure and, 19
Digital Curation Centre's (DCC) Data Curation Lifecycle Model, 26
digital enablers, 46, 46
digital leadership: advocacy by, 12–15, 45, 46; collection teams in, 43–44; digital strategy by, 35–37; institution

Index ~ 91

unity in, 36; organizational structures in, 41
digital-preservation: back-up vs., 74; in digital stewardship, xii, xiv–xv, 1, 3, 9; early intervention, unified approach and, 3, 11–12, 53–54; NDSA and, 26–27, 72; NIST cloud models for, 77–78; OAIS model in, 4, 25–26, 63–64; security in, 73, 80–83; storage costs in, 29, 76, 82–84; storage in, 71–74; system architecture of, 74–75; tiered-storage strategies for, 54, 78–80, 79. *See also* cloud-based digital preservation storage
Digital Preservation Capacity Maturity Model (DPCMM), 27
Digital Preservation Coalition Rapid Assessment Model (DPC-RAM), 27
Digital Repository Audit Method Based in Risk Assessment (DRAMBORA), 27
digital repository certification, 25–26
digital rights management: as DAME component, 8, 13; as digital stewardship component, 9, 13; safeguard of, 14
digital stewardship: administration in, 10–11; cloud-based storage in, 71–84; core conceptual models of, 65; cost modeling in, 29–30; DAME in, 11; data curation in, xii–xiv, 1, 3, 9; digital asset ecosystem in, 6–8, 7; digital leadership in, 36–37; digital preservation in, xii, xiv–xv, 1, 3, 9; digital rights management component, 9, 13; digitization in, 9, 60–61, 60–63; DPCMM in, 27; framework of, xii, xiii, 6–11, 7, 9; functional gaps in, 10, 19; GLAM in, xii, 19–20; IG, digital advocacy and, 12–15, 45, 46; institutional support for, 13–14; integrative collections management in, 51–66; metadata component, 9; partnerships in, xv, 1–3, 11; principles guiding, 5–11; professional development in, 45–46, 46; RDM in, 64–65; records and information management component in, 9; risk-management assessment, 28; roles, responsibilities and, 11–12; service model of, 6; social responsibility in, 11; sustainability in, xii, xiii, 8–9, 9, 26, 54–55, 71, 84–85; team building in, 32; tools for, xiv–xv; unstructured data in, 28–30
digital stewardship assessment: analysis and prioritized recommendations of, 30–31; benefits of, 20–21, 28; exit strategies in, 28; GLAM approach to, 19–20; as holistic, xii, xiii, 8–9, 9, 19–32, 51–53; obstacles in, 19, 28; report of, 31–32; segmentation of, 22, 22–25; as technical infrastructure strategy, 21
digital strategy, xiii; as cloud tiered storage, 54, 78–80, 79; collection restructuring in, 37; digital leadership in, 35–37; for digital preservation, 54; functions of, 10; for GLAM institutions, 35–36, 51, 84–85; infrastructure integration as, 38; as integrative collections management, 51, 55; new organizational program models for, 40–41; phased approach to, 35–47; primary analysis for, 23–24; professional development in, 44–47, 46; realignment, xiii, 35–37, 44–47, 46. *See also* realignment
digitization: analog archival processing to mass, 58–59; analog collections path to, 60–61, 60–63; as digital stewardship component, 9; fund models for, 62–63; RFP for, 62
direct attached storage (DAS), 75
discovery platforms, 65–66
distinctive collections, 42–44
distributed service architecture, 1, 37
DPCMM. *See* Digital Preservation Capacity Maturity Model

DPCRAM. *See* Digital Preservation Coalition Rapid Assessment Model
DPM Maturity Model, 26
DRAMBORA. *See* Digital Repository Audit Method Based in Risk Assessment
DSA. *See* Data Seal of Approval

egress charges, 83
enterprise infrastructure, 38
exit strategies, 28, 83–84

Freedom of Information Act (FOIA), 14
functional specialists, 42–43
funding: digitization models for, 62–63; of GLAM, 6, 36–37

galleries, libraries, archives and museums (GLAM): challenges of, 51–52; cloud-based storage of, 71–84; cross-functional workflows in, 56–58, 57; DAME advocacy for, 12–15, 45, 46, 66; DAME in, xi; digital collections of, xi–xiii, 1; digital leadership of, 35–37; digital stewardship of, xii, 19–20; digital strategy in, 35, 51; digitization path for, 60–61, 60–63; fund interests of, 6, 36–37; infrastructure development, modular design and, 37–40; infrastructure scalability in, 21, 37–40; initiatives of, xii; integrity monitoring in, 73; internal environmental scan in, 23; investment of, 10–12, 14, 37–38; IT, collections-management system and, 52–53; open access support by, 66; organizational program model for, 40–41; organizational restructuring in, 40–41, 44–47, 46; personnel realignment in, 42–43; RFP in, 62; social responsibility of, 11, 84–85; staff of, xi, xiv; strategy of, 36, 51, 84–85; technology of, xii
geographic information systems (GIS), 6

GLAM. *See* galleries, libraries, archives and museums
graphic replication, 73
Greene, Mark, 58–59

holistic assessment: department convergence in, 51–53; of digital stewardship, xii, *xiii*, 8–9, 9, 19–32

IEC. *See* International Electrotechnical Commission
IG. *See* information governance
ILS. *See* integrated library system
information governance (IG): digital stewardship and, 12–15, 45, 46; executive sponsor of, 13; as organization management, 12–13
information repositories, 5, 21
information technology (IT): collections-management system convergence with, 52–53; departments in, 39–40; integrative collections management, convergence and, 51–53
infrastructure development and modular design: as digital strategy, 38; in GLAM, 37–40; interoperability in, 38–39; realignment for, 37–40
infrastructure platforms: as discovery platform, 65–66; LSA as, 3; technical, 19, 21, 37–40
infrastructure scalability, 21, 37–40
institutional repositories (IR): application programming interfaces for, 5, 21; as DAME component, 4–5; DPM Maturity Model in, 26; security in, 7; TRAC for, 25–26
integrated library system (ILS) development, 2
integrative collections management, *xii*, 40–41; analog archival processing to strategic mass digitization, 58–59; cross-functional workflows, curation ready assets and, 55–58, 57; definition of, 54–55; digital

preservation, early intervention and, 3, 11–12, 53–54; in digital stewardship, 51–66; digital strategy in, 51, 55; digitization path for, 60–61, 60–63; diverse discovery platforms in, 65–66; examples of, 55; IT convergence and, 51–53; monograph cataloging, metadata harvesting, remediation and, 63–64; research data, digital archives and, 64–65
integrity monitoring, 73
internal environmental scan, 22, 23
International Electrotechnical Commission (IEC), 72
International Organization for Standardization (ISO), 72
internet protocol (IP), 73
interoperability, 38–39
investment strategy: of GLAM, 10–12, 14, 37–38; ROI in, 12, 14
IP. *See* internet protocol
IR. *See* institutional repositories
ISO. *See* International Organization for Standardization
IT. *See* information technology

library catalog, 2
library service platform (LSA) systems, 3
lifecycle management, xii; DCC model for, 26; intervention in, 3, 11–12, 53–54; OAIS model in, 4, 25–26, 63–64; range of, 10–11; stakeholders in, 12
linear tape-open (LTO) storage, 74–75
LSA. *See* library service platform
LTO. *See* linear tape-open

machine-readable catalog (MARC), 58
MAM. *See* media asset management
MARC. *See* machine-readable catalog
master data management (MDM), 5
media asset management (MAM), 38
Meissner, Dennis, 58–59

metadata: as digital asset conveyor, 7; as digital stewardship component, 9; in integrative collections management, 63–64; OAI for, 63; OAI-PMH for, 63–64; as value added service, 10
modular design. *See* infrastructure development and modular design
"More Product, Less Process" (Green and Meissner), 58–59

NARA. *See* National Archives and Records Administration
NAS. *See* networked attached storage
National Archives and Records Administration (NARA), 3–4
National Digital Stewardship Alliance's (NDSA) Levels of Preservation: digital preservation matrix for, 26–27; storage requirements of, 72
National Institute of Standards and Technology (NIST): cloud computing characteristics defined by, 76; storage deployment models defined by, 77–78
NDSA. *See* National Digital Stewardship Alliance's (NDSA) Levels of Preservation
networked attached storage (NAS), 75
NIST. *See* National Institute of Standards and Technology

OAI. *See* Open Archives Initiative
OAI-PMH. *See* Open Archives Initiatives Protocol for Metadata Harvesting
OAIS. *See* Open Archival Information System
OCR. *See* optical reader recognition
online library system, 2
open access, 64, 66
Open Archival Information System (OAIS): as digital lifecycle management model, 4, 25–26, 63–64; in PARS, 4; storage requirements in, 72

Open Archives Initiative (OAI), 63
Open Archives Initiatives Protocol for Metadata Harvesting (OAI-PMH), 63–64
optical character recognition (OCR), 62
organizational management, 40–41, 44–47, 46; IG as, 12–13. *See also* digital strategy; realignment

PARS. *See* Preservation and Reformatting Section Working Group
pay-as-you-go cost, 76, 82
PDI. *See* preservation descriptive information
Preservation and Reformatting Section (PARS) Working Group, 4
preservation descriptive information (PDI), 63
primary collection analysis, 22, 23–24
professional development, 44–47, 46

RDM. *See* research data management
realignment: capacity building component of, 36–37; as continuum, 21; digital strategy and, xiii, 35–37, 44–47, 46; for distinctive collections, 43–44; infrastructure development, modular design and, 37–40; IT, collections management and, 51–53; organization development as, 40–41, 44–47, 46; subject curators to functional specialists, 42–43. *See also* digital strategy
records and information management, 9
redundancy, 73, 75, 83
remediation, 63–64
representative information (RI), 63
request for proposal (RFP), 62
research data management (RDM), 64–65
return on investment (ROI), 12, 14
RFP. *See* request for proposal

RI. *See* representative information
risk-management assessment, 27, 28
ROI. *See* return on investment

SAN. *See* storage architecture network
scalability, 21, 37–40
scale: of DAME, xii–xiv, 1; of digital asset, 19; of unstructured data, 28–29
security: audit trails as, 73; in cloud-based digital preservation data storage, 80–83; in IR, 7; standards, 72
service level agreement (SLA), 82
significant properties, 7
silo. *See* collection silo
SLA. *See* service level agreement
social responsibility, 11, 84–85
storage. *See* cloud-based digital preservation storage
storage architecture network (SAN), 75
subject curators, 42–43
sustainability: in digital stewardship, xii, xiii, 8–9, 9, 26, 54–55, 71, 84–85; of GLAM, 36, 84–85

TCO. *See* total cost of ownership
technical infrastructure, xii; assessment as strategy for, 21; digital collections and, 19; scalability in, 21, 37–40
tier-based storage, 54, 78–80, 79
total cost of ownership (TCO), 29
TRAC. *See* Trustworthy Repositories Audit and Certification Criteria and Checklist
Trustworthy Repositories Audit and Certification Criteria and Checklist (TRAC): for digital repositories, 25–26; storage requirements of, 72

unit of information, 7
unstructured data, 28–30

workflows. *See* cross-functional workflows

About the Author

Angela Fritz is state archivist and division administrator for Library, Archives, and Museum Collections (LAMC) at the Wisconsin Historical Society. In this capacity, she provides strategic direction and oversight for museum curation, archives, library administration, public services, collection development, collection management, preservation, conservation, digitization, and the historical government records program. Prior to her position at the Wisconsin Historical Society, Dr. Fritz served as head of the University of Notre Dame Archives and interim head of Special Collections and University Archives at the University of Arkansas in Fayetteville. Her previous experience also includes working as an archivist for the Office of Presidential Libraries and Museums in Washington, DC where she engaged in presidential library development on behalf of the National Archives and Records Administration. She has a PhD in American history and public history from Loyola University Chicago, where she was awarded a Crown Fellowship in the humanities. She holds a master's degree in library science with a concentration in archival administration from the University of Wisconsin-Madison.

www.ingramcontent.com/pod-product-compliance
Lightning Source LLC
Chambersburg PA
CBHW052051300426
44117CB00012B/2081